HAVE A BLAST BOOKING AND PERFORMING GIGS FOR THE MODERN MUSICIAN

Visit GigBookingSecrets.com And Download The Free Forms Kit

10 Fun Mastery Workshops For Musicians

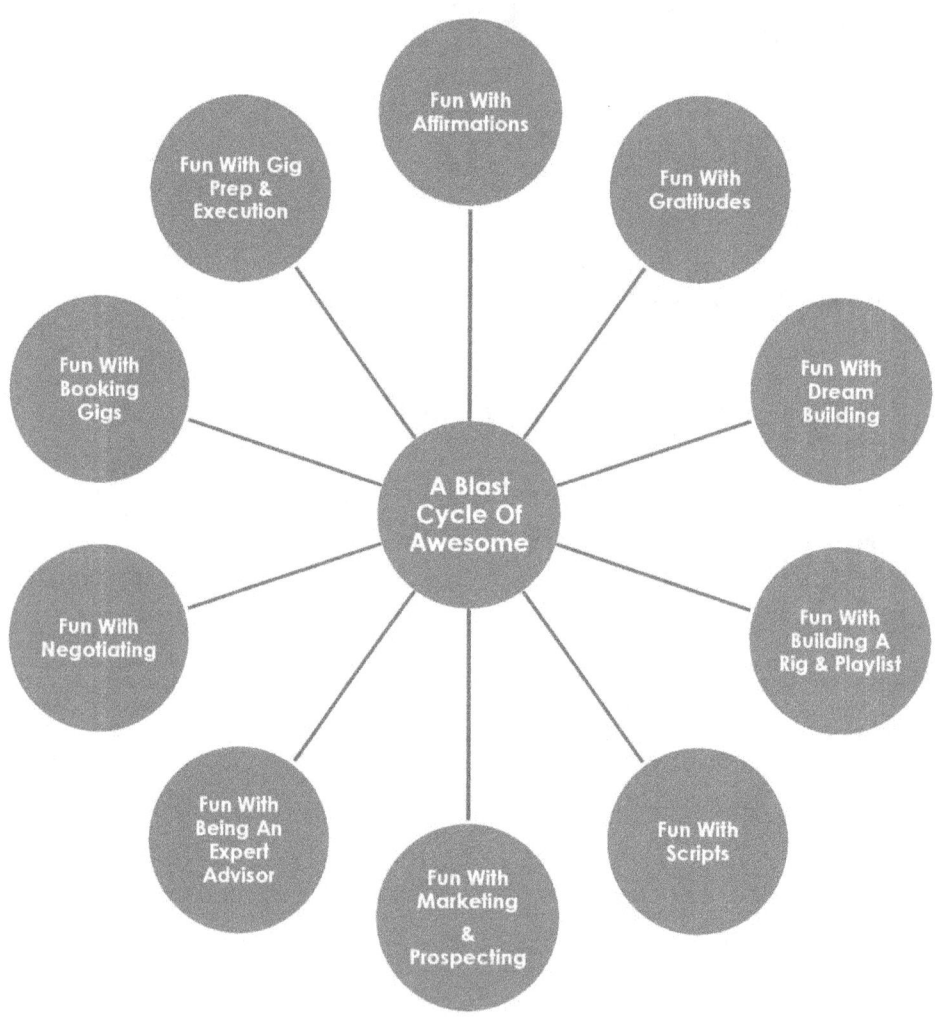

Opinions and recommendations given herein are based on the author's experience and on research believed accurate and reliable but not infallible. It should be stated that the principles mentioned in this book were chosen only to demonstrate a given point or points. The reader must necessarily act under his or her own responsibility.

All rights reserved. No part of this book may be reproduced, distributed, or transmitted in any form or by any electronic or mechanical means including information storage and retrieval systems except in the case of brief quotations in articles or reviews without the permission in writing from the publisher.

All brand names and product names used in this book are trademarks, registered trademarks, or trade names of their respective holders. I am not associated with any product or vendor in this book.

Copyright ©2018 Rick Sanford
Have A Blast Publishing
All Rights Reserved
ISBN 978-0-692-04764-4 eBook
ISBN 978-0-692-10342-5 paperback
For permission requests, write to the publisher at the address below.
3780 Old Norcross Road Suite 103-326
Duluth Georgia 30096

Contents

Why I Wrote This Book 6
Introducing The A Blast Cycle of Awesome 8
Workshop 1 Fun With Affirmations 10
Workshop 2 Fun With Gratitudes 26
Workshop 3 Fun With Dream Building 31
Workshop 4 Fun With Building A Rig And Playlist 35
Workshop 5 Fun With Scripts 44
Workshop 6 Fun With Prospecting And Marketing 54
Workshop 7 Fun With Being An Expert Advisor 67
Workshop 8 Fun With Negotiating 82
Workshop 9 Fun With Booking Gigs 90
Workshop 10 Fun With Gig Prep And Execution 102
About The Author 127
More From This Author 129
One Last Thing 130

Dedicated To The

World's Musicians

Fun Mastery And Harmonious

Living Begins Today

Why I Wrote This Book

Thanks for investing in this book; my name is Rick Sanford founder of A Blast Bands And DJs®, co-founder/guitarist of The Blast Band® and author of this fun and crazy training program for the modern musician. I wrote this book for several reasons. The first is to teach every musician on the planet how to book and perform gigs so they can live a life full of music, fun, love and money.

The second reason is to share our A Blast story of transformation. I personally didn't know anything about getting a gig when starting out and since then have accumulated three decades of experience, wisdom and knowledge on this valuable subject. The final reason I wrote this book is to kick off our training programs focusing on the development, encouragement and wellness for musicians around the globe!

Our music service, A Blast Bands And DJs®, is based in Atlanta Georgia and we've had the privilege of performing for thousands of customers around the United States. It's been an amazing time sharing our talents, passion and expertise while generating revenue making customers happy. This book will show you how we did it with our formulas, systems and methodologies found in the A Blast Cycle of Awesome framework I put together for you!

It all started in 1987; when I had to take a leap of faith! I was not happy in the corporate world and decided to make a lifestyle change. My passions have always been rooted in music playing guitar, singing, being in bands, writing songs and making people happy so I decided to launch a music service starting out as a one-man band and build from there.

Being a full-time musician was kind of scary at first but with the help of some mindset strategies covered in the first three workshops, I was able to convince myself to stay committed to my new career. Most musicians are looking for three things... an exciting life, gigs in the books and money in the bank. You can have all three if you learn the material within these pages.

I feel honored and privileged to be your guide as I walk you through the A Blast Cycle of Awesome framework. I hope you enjoy this information as much as I did creating it for you. Please take advantage of the information by doing the homework assignments so you too can go forth, serve and have a blast booking and performing gigs!

Rick Sanford

Introducing The A Blast Cycle of Awesome

How Do You Become An Expert At Booking And Performing Gigs? Simply Learn These Ten Workshops! The A Blast Cycle of Awesome is a simple to follow framework I created consisting of ten-workshops that shows musicians how to become experts at booking and performing gigs.

Each workshop is introduced in the order that I pretty much had to learn them as time went by. The first three workshops, the fundamentals, are focused on building solid mindset habits while the remaining seven cover conceptual and tactical strategies that will help you earn your way to success quickly.

We're going to start at the top of the cycle and go clockwise drilling down on each subject. I've also included workshop assignments, so you can sharpen your skills in no time at all.

You just might end up living a joyful, harmonious life with lots of gigs in the books that pay well... for at least the next 30 years! You deserve it... so why not get started today!

The A Blast Cycle Of Awesome

Workshop 1 Fun With Affirmations

Let's all brainwash ourselves for better living, shall we? In this workshop, I will show you how to become an affirmations expert so you can control your thoughts for the absolute best life possible! I'm sure you will agree with me that the world is trying to knock you off your game every minute so combat it by creating your own customized affirmations list. It will help flush away negative thinking and eliminate the junk we all love to accumulate in our minds. This simple act will free up resources, so you can start living life guilt free and joyful like you deserve!

When I decided to start a music service way back in 1987, about 70% of my thoughts were negative. That positive-negative thought ratio was totally unacceptable to me if I was going to be successful at my new musical venture. I decided to go out and rent/buy a bunch of self-help books, tapes and cd's to fix this challenge. After reviewing the programs, I noticed that they all had one common thread running through them... positive affirmations!

Because of these findings, I simply created a bunch of A Blast Affirmations (any positive statement with "It's fun" in front of it) to trick out my brain and keep thoughts positive most of the time. The ultimate goal I set for myself was to make 99% of my daily thoughts positive and 1% negative. Amazingly, this simple technique has worked great for me and that's why I am asking you to try it out for yourself! You will love the results!

Bottom line, selective brainwashing is one of the secrets to a happy life! Simply start a journal, grab these mini pep rallies, practice them daily and become an affirmations expert in a matter of weeks!There's no telling what your life is going to be like in a few months... but I bet you will be experiencing better living!

Workshop Instructions:

1. Review the following affirmations.

2. Pick the ones you like and put them in your journal.

3. Customize the list by altering and adding your own personal touches.

4. Refer to them twice a day, in the morning and at night for 21 days then once a day thereafter. As an option, say them out loud for extra impact.

5. For best results, record them over your favorite tunes! Daily review is the key to getting the most out of this workshop so please do not skip this part of the training. It will help you book and perform more gigs!

A Blast Affirmations

It's fun having **A Blast** today and everyday!
It's fun helping others have **A Blast**!
It's fun having a life full of **Abundance**!
It's fun **Accepting** myself for who I am, a unique individual with many talents!
It's fun knowing what **Accomplishment** feels like!
It's fun overcoming fear with **Action**!
It's fun alternating between right and left brain **Activities** throughout the day!
It's fun going over positive **Affirmations** regularly!
It's fun being **Ambitious**!
It's fun avoiding **Anger**!
It's fun transforming **Anxiety** into peace of mind!
It's fun not making **Apologies** for who I am and what I do!
It's fun having a positive and joyful **Attitude**!
It's fun having a 'will do, can do' **Attitude**!
It's fun having a forgive and forget **Attitude**!
It's fun **Believing** in myself!
It's fun knowing that I am equal to the **Best**!
It's fun knowing that my **Best Days** are ahead of me!
It's fun reading the world's greatest sales manual, **The Bible**!
It's fun being **Blessed**!
It's fun **Booking & Performing Gigs**!
It's fun selectively **Brainwashing** myself for better living!
It's fun being **Brilliant**!
It's fun succeeding in **Business**!
It's fun only doing **Business** with people that want to do business with me!
It's fun handing out **Business Cards** to everyone!
It's fun generating **Cash Flow**!

It's fun accepting **Challenges** calmly and in good spirit!
It's fun having **30 Day Challenges** every month!
It's fun accepting **Change**!
It's fun helping others **Change** their lives for the better!
It's fun giving to the causes that I most **Care** about!
It's fun supporting, promoting and serving a great local **Charity**! Looking for one? Visit childrn.org
It's fun being **Cheerful**!
It's fun supporting my local **Church**! Looking for one? Visit 12stone.com
It's fun creating possitive **Circumstances**!
It's fun being **Coachable**!
It's fun being and excellent **Communicator**!
It's fun having **Compassion** for others!
It's fun being **Complimentary** to others for the excellent work they do!
It's fun giving back to the **Community**!
It's fun reaching out to the **Community** and selling our products and services!
It's fun having **Composure** always regardless of the situation!
It's fun having **Concern for Others**!
It's fun being **Confident**!
It's fun being in **Control** of my life!
It's fun being **Courageous** because I know action always beats fear!
It's fun being **Courteous** to those who offer criticism!
It's fun being **Creative**! Creative people are the happiest people on earth; I spend several hours each day in my creative space.
It's fun learning from constructive **Criticism!**
It's fun talking to **Customers** on the phone, they warm up to me like an old friend!
It's fun anticipating the needs of **Customers**!
It's fun knowing the value of posting and sharing our **Customer Reviews**!

It's fun practicing my instrument **Daily** because it's the only way to greatness!
It's fun staying out of political **Debate**!
It's fun avoiding **Depression**!
It's fun knowing my true **Desires**!
It's fun having **Destiny**!
It's fun having **Discipline** in my life!
It's fun **Discovering** everything good life has to offer!
It's fun being **Diverse**!
It's fun **Donating** to those less fortunate than myself!
It's fun starving my **Doubts**!
It's fun having a **Dream Book**! I refer to it often because with proper planning, hard work and a little luck… dreams do come true!
It's fun having a **Dream Job**!
It's fun feeding my **Dreams**!
It's fun focusing and working on my **Dreams** daily!
It's fun throwing money at my **Dreams**!
It's fun being **Efficient**!
It's fun showing my true **Emotions** as they arise!
It's fun feeling **Empowered**!
It's fun **Encouraging** myself and others!
It's fun having an **Enemy**! (Broke is the enemy)
It's fun being full of youthful **Energy**!
It's fun being **Energized**!
It's fun being **Enthusiastic** about where I'm going, and what I am doing!
It's fun being an **Entrepreneur**!
It's fun avoiding **Envy,** it has no place in my life!
It's fun writing my own **Eulogy,** so I know that someone doesn't screw it up!
It's fun living an **Exciting Life**!
It's fun creating an **Excuse Sheet,** so I can read it when I'm feeling unmotivated!

It's fun having a sensible **Exercise** routine! I work out at least three times a week. I have never felt better!
It's fun **Experiencing More** in life, I certainly deserve it!
It's fun being an **Expert** in my chosen field!
It's fun working with a team of talented **Experts**!
It's fun documenting the **Extraordinary** in my journal!
It's fun owning a **'Faith It Out'** attitude!
It's fun taking care of my **Family**!
It's fun devoting at least one day a week to my **Family**.
It's fun having **Family Gatherings** regularly!
It's fun being a **Fighter** when there's good reason!
It's fun knowing that it's not the size of the dog in the **Fight** but the size of the **Fight** in the dog!
It's fun reaching my **Financial Goals**!
It's fun being a **Finisher**! I hang in there with what I set out to do regardless of the odds!
It's fun earning **Five Star Reviews** with my customers!
It's fun staying **Focused** on my dream!
It's fun knowing the right **Foods** to eat! I choose to live a healthy lifestyle. I make healthy choices, pay attention to portions and keep nutrition in mind.
It's fun having a **Follow-Up System** with all my customers!
It's fun having a detailed **Forecast** for my life... 1, 3, 5, 7+ years out!
It's fun having **Foresight** to get things done! My daily and weekly planner keeps me on track!
It's fun attracting good **Fortune** in my life!
It's fun being **Free** to do as I choose!
It's fun being **Friendly And Outgoing**!
It's fun being **Generous**!
It's fun being **Generous** at praising others!
It's fun performing high paying **Gigs**!
It's fun having defined daily, weekly, monthly and yearly **Goals**!
It's fun having realistic **Goals** and direction!

It's fun having **God Size Dreams**!
It's fun not taking people for **Granted**!
It's fun creating and reviewing my **Gratitude List** regularly!
It's fun not being **Greedy** because pigs get fat and hogs get slaughtered!
It's fun avoiding **Grief**!
It's fun being **Guilt Free**!
It's fun replacing bad **Habits** with good ones!
It's fun being a **HAM**! (**H**appy **A**live **M**otivated)
It's fun being one of the **Happiest** people on earth!
It's fun knowing that I can build **Happiness** one thought at a time!
It's fun making people **Happy**!
It's fun living in **Harmony**!
It's fun having amazing **Health**!
It's fun guarding my **Health**!
It's fun being **Healthy**!
It's fun following my **Heart**!
It's fun **Helping** others less fortunate than myself!
It's fun being **Honest** with myself and therefore with everyone else!
It's fun staying **Hydrated** by drinking a gallon of water each day! I have replaced moisture zapping caffeinated beverages.
It's fun being **Image** conscious!
It's fun being **imaginative**!
It's fun having a strong and vibrant **Immune System**!
It's fun **Improving** my life!
It's fun knowing that I will never need to worry about a steady **Income**!
It's fun being **Independent** of another person's opinion!
It's fun being **Inspired**!
It's fun covering my assets by having all my instruments and gear **Insured** against theft!
It's fun being **Intelligent**!

It's fun being **Interested** in other people rather than talk about myself!
It's fun being an **Inverse Paranoid**!
It's fun **Investing** in people!
It's fun **Investing** in myself! The better I become, the better everything around me becomes!
It's fun **Innovating**!
It's fun having **Integrity**! I'll never sacrifice it!
It's fun having good **Intentions** in my life!
It's fun asking, "What would **Jesus** do?" in all situations!
It's fun having a **Journal** to write in and refer to daily! It helps solve many challenges in my life!
It's fun **Journaling**! Magical things happen when I put pen to paper!
It's fun knowing that God gave us **Joy**, we have a right to perfect it!
It's fun bringing **Joy** to others!
It's fun being a **Joy Bringer**!
It's fun being **Joyful**!
It's fun not **Judging** others!
It's fun being **Kind**!
It's fun **Laughing** out loud!
It's fun being a **Leap of Faith** individual!
It's fun being a **Learner**!
It's fun scheduling **Leisure** time!
It's fun breaking down self-imposed **Limitations**!
It's fun being an excellent **Listener**!
It's fun **Living** in the now!
It's fun living a life filled with **Love**!
It's fun doing what I **Love**!
It's fun being **Loved**!
It's fun being a **Loving** person!
It's fun being **Loyal**!
It's fun being a **Lucky** person!
It's fun attracting **Good Luck** into my life!

It's fun creating **Magic** through music!
It's fun having what it takes to **Make It** in this world!
It's fun having effective **Marketing** campaigns!
It's fun building a better **Me**!
It's fun having **Mental Toughness**!
It's fun having a **Mentor**!
It's fun being a **Mentor**!
It's fun feeling like a **Million Bucks**!
It's fun having a youthful **Mindset**!
It's fun looking in the mirror and seeing a **Miracle**!
It's fun having a **Mission** in life!
It's fun having a **Mission Statement**!
It's fun forgetting yet learning from my **Mistakes**!
It's fun being **Motivated**!
It's fun **Motivating** others!
It's fun being a full time **Musician**!
It's fun striving to be the best **Musician** possible!
It's fun looking after and taking care of **Musicians**!
It's fun supporting local **Musicians**!
It's fun not second guessing **Myself**!
It's fun tuning out the **Naysayers**!
It's fun omitting **Negative Messaging** in my life!
It's fun avoiding **Negative** people!
It's fun flushing away my **Negative Thoughts**. They are gone with the wind!
It's fun crushing my **Negative Thoughts** by writing them down, thinking about it, crossing through it and writing down what I really think!
It's fun perfecting the art and science of **Negotiating** with my customers. I make it an enjoyable, lighthearted experience.
It's fun not giving into a **Nervous Breakdown** a.k.a. the devils baptism!
It's fun **Networking** with other professionals!

It's fun waking up the 80 trillion **Neurons** I have laying around in my body simply waiting for instructions.
It's fun tuning out the daily **News**! I have eliminated negative thought activities in my life!
It's fun expressing my **Opinions** easily!
It's fun having unlimited **Opportunities**!
It's fun tuning-in to the **Opportunities** that surround me!
It's fun being an **Optimist**!
It's fun having unshakable **Optimism** about myself and others!
It's fun knowing the **Optimist Creed** by Christian D. Larson!
It's fun being **Organized**!
It's fun being **Outgoing**!
It's fun **Owning** a home! Buying 'Subject To' is awesome!
It's fun choosing **Pain** over regret! Regret has no room in my life!
It's fun living my **Passion**!
It's fun being **Passionate** towards others!
It's fun letting go of the **Past**! The past is gone!
It's fun having **Patience**!
It's fun having **Peace of Mind**!
It's fun having interest in other **People**!
It's fun having **Perseverance**!
It's fun being **Persistent**!
It's fun being a **No Limit Person**!
It's fun breaking **Personal Records** mentally, spiritually and physically!
It's fun having a caring **Personality**!
It's fun working my daily and weekly **Planner**!
It's fun **Planning** great things! My best days are ahead of me!
It's fun being **Positive**!
It's fun having my **Prayers** answered!
It's fun **Praying** for the world's musicians!
It's fun being **Proactive** rather than reactive!
It's fun finding, facing and fighting my **Problems**!
It's fun eliminating **Procrastination**!

It's fun being **Productive**!
It's fun **Prospecting** for new customers daily!
It's fun creating and signing my own **Prosperity Oath**!
It's fun being a **Prosperity Pusher**!
It's fun knowing that I have the right to be **Prosperous**!
It's fun knowing my **Purpose** in life!
It's fun working for **Quality**!
It's fun delivering the finest **Quality** to my customers!
It's fun **Reading** one new book a month!
It's fun having the power to create my **Reality**!
It's fun **Rehearsing** before each gig!
It's fun letting music be my **Religion**!
It's fun being a **Renegade**!
It's fun doing **Research**! I enjoy learning new things and keep an open mind on how to apply the newfound knowledge to my life!
Its fun avoiding **Resentment**!
It's fun being **Respectful** toward others!
It's fun continuously developing as a **Resource**!
It's fun freeing up **Resources** in my life for things that matter!
It's fun being well **Rested** for optimal performance!
It's fun staying focused on **Results**!
It's fun generating **Revenue**! I love it when folks smile, say "thank you" and hand me a check!
It's fun being **Rich** on the inside!
It's fun being **Rich** on the outside!
It's fun keeping my **Rig** in tip top shape for the best performance possible!
It's fun being blessed with the ability to **Rock Out** anytime and anywhere!
It's fun breaking the **Rules**! Not the law, the rules.
It's fun being one of the world's greatest **Salespeople**!
It's fun having a harmonious work **Schedule**. I spend half my time on creative things and half my time on administrative things.

It's fun creating a pictorial **Scrapbook** of my life, so I can see how much I've grown year after year!
It's fun avoiding **Self-Defeating** thoughts!
It's fun having **Self-Discipline**!
It's fun being **Self-Educating**!
It's fun working on my **Self-Improvement** daily!
It's fun being a **Self-Starter**!
It's fun being **Self-Sufficient**!
It's fun having positive **Self-Talk** 99% of the time!
It's fun **Selling** products and services that sell themselves!
It's fun providing the highest quality **Service** possible to my customers!
It's fun **Serving** others!
It's fun **Sharing** what I have with others!
It's fun **Singing** at the top of my lungs when I'm onstage!
It's fun knowing the value of a **Smile**, I have a mirror at my desk to remind me that it goes right through the phone.
It's fun having great **Social Skills**!
It's fun focusing on **Solutions** and not problems!
It's fun creating win-win **Solutions** with my family, friends, co-workers and customers!
It's fun easily **Speaking** with people I've just met!
It's fun being a **Stress-Free** person!
It's fun doing light **Stretching** before work sessions and gigs. Sprains/injuries have no room in my life!
It's fun knowing that I do not need anyone's permission to **Succeed**!
It's fun being **Successful**!
It's fun knowing that I have a right to be **Successful**!
It's fun remembering my **Successes** and forgetting my failures!
It's fun building **Systems** that work for me in my situation!
It's fun developing my **Talents**!
It's fun being easy to **Talk** to!
It's fun having **Targets & Timelines** in my life!

It's fun keeping up with my **Tax Obligations**!
It's fun **Teaching** others what I know!
It's fun knowing the power of a **Team**! (**T**ogether **E**veryone **A**chieves **M**ore)
It's fun being empowered through **Teamwork**!
It's fun turning off the **Television**!
It's fun living life on my **Terms**!
It's fun avoiding self defeating **Thoughts**!
It's fun thinking rich pure **Thoughts** all day!
It's fun being **Thick Skinned**!
It's fun spending my **Time** wisely!
It's fun being a **Time Management** expert!
It's fun **Treating** others like I would like to be treated!
It's fun being a **Trend Setter**!
It's fun feeling **Triumphant**!
It's fun being **Trustworthy**!
It's fun being **Unique**!
It's fun being **Unpredictable**!
It's fun being **Unstoppable**!
It's fun providing the finest **Value** to my customers!
It's fun knowing the **Value of Empty**!
It's fun being **Vibrant**!
It's fun being **Wealthy** in every area of my life!
It's fun staying close to my ideal **Weight**. I stay 10% above or 5% below this range for optimal health.
It's fun having a written **Will** to help loved ones out when I'm transferred to heaven!
It's fun having a **Winner Mentality**!
It's fun keeping my **Word**!
It's fun choosing my **Words** carefully!
It's fun **Tuning Out The World**!
It's fun being a **Worker**! Extra-effort always produces the best results!
It's fun avoiding **Worry**!

It's fun **Writing** songs!
It's fun saying **'YES I CAN!'** out loud!
It's fun growing **Younger**!
It's fun having **Zest** in my life!
It's fun having **Zeal** in my life!

Congratulations On Working Up Your Affirmations List!

How Many Did You End Up With?

Do Not Pass Go Until You Know! Mind Jail Is A Horrible Thing To Live With So Make Your List Today!

Notes And Thoughts

Notes And Thoughts

Workshop 2 Fun With Gratitudes

Let's all count our lucky stars, shall we? In this workshop I will show you how to be a gratitude expert so you can live a joyful life without being envious of others or getting caught up in the "Kingdom of Thingdom" syndrome the world loves to push on all of us.

This workshop came about because several years ago, I was curious about how many blessings I had in my life and started to write them down. After working on the list for several days, I decided to alphabetize them.

I couldn't believe it, I counted 143 things I was thankful for! It made me feel great about my life and that's why I am asking you to try out this technique for yourself! Believe me, you will love how you feel once you make your list and review it!

Simply give yourself several days to put them all down, alphabetize them and review them regularly.

You just might end up with a perfectly tailored list of everything you're thankful for... thus making you a gratitude expert! It will help you book and perform more gigs!

Workshop Instructions:

1. Review the following gratitude statements.

2. Pick out the ones you like and put them in your journal.

3. Customize the list by adding your own personal touches.

4. Refer to them twice a day, in the morning and at night, for 21 days then once a day thereafter. Say them out loud for extra impact.

5. For best results, record them over your favorite tunes!

Gratitude Statements

I'm thankful I've worked up **Affirmations** for my life!
I am thankful for being **Bold**!
I'm grateful for having trustworthy **Business** partners!
I am thankful for having **Customers** who appreciate quality!
I'm thankful for having **Discipline** in my life!
I am grateful for being a skilled **Entertainer**!
I'm thankful that I am an **Entrepreneur**!
I am grateful for having **Faith**!
I'm thankful for being **Fearless**!
I am grateful for having the ability to **Forgive**!
I'm thankful for being **Free**!
I'm thankful for having a **Free Spirit**!
I am grateful for having **Friends** I can trust!
I am grateful for the **Gigs** we have in the books!
I'm thankful for the **Goals** I have!
I'm thankful for being a **Guitar Player**!
I'm grateful for having a **Happy Life**!
I am grateful for having a big **Heart**!
I'm grateful for having a nice **Home**!
I am thankful for being an **Honest Person**!
I am thankful for being a person of **Integrity**!
I'm grateful for having **Intelligence**!
I'm grateful for being a **Joyful Person**!
I am thankful that my brain is **Junk Free**!
I am grateful for having **Leadership Skills**!
I am thankful for being **Loyal** to those who depend on me!
I'm thankful for having **Managerial Skills**!

I am thankful for having **Marketing Skills**!
I'm thankful for having a **Mission**!
I am grateful for being a **Motivator**!
I'm grateful for being a **Musician**!
I'm grateful for having Expert **Musicians** in my life!
I'm thankful for having great **Negotiating Skills**!
I am thankful for having an **Optimized Life**!
I am grateful for having **Organizational Skills**!
I am grateful to have wonderful **Parents**!
I am grateful to have **Peace of Mind**!
I'm thankful for being **Persistent**!
I'm grateful for having the ability to **Protect My Loved Ones**!
I'm thankful for being a good **Researcher**!
I am grateful for being **Rich** in every aspect of my life!
I am thankful for having **Self Respect**!
I'm thankful for having the ability to **Serve**!
I am grateful for having wonderful **Siblings**!
I'm thankful for having the ability to **Sing**!
I am grateful for the **Stagehands** in my life!
I'm thankful for having **Talent**!
I am thankful for being a **Teacher**!
I'm grateful for having a great **Team** to work with!
I am thankful for having **Versatility**!
I am thankful for being **Victorious**!
I'm grateful for having a **Vision** for the future!
I am thankful for being a **Worry-Free** person!

Congratulations On Working Up Your Customized Gratitude List!

So How Many Did You End Up With?

Notes And Thoughts

Notes And Thoughts

Workshop 3 Fun With Dream Building

Let's document our dreams, work hard on them and watch them come true, shall we? In this third fundamental workshop, I will show you how to be an expert dream builder for better living! Creating a dreams list is an amazing and magical thing because it forces your brain to focus on things you want in life and repel against that which you do not.

Here's how it works! Simply write down a dream you have in detail, add an image and a proposed achievement date. Make sure you use words like I am, I own, I have, I enjoy, etc. in past tence... like they have already happened.

With hard work and a little luck, you just might end up living the life of your dreams simply because you took the time to define them! It's one of the secrets to a happy life plus it will help you book and perform more gigs!

Workshop Instructions:

1. Create a detailed list of everything you are dreaming about.

2. Add a photo if you wish.

3. Alphabetize them and put them in your journal.

4. Refer to them twice a day, in the morning and at night, for 21 days then once a day thereafter. Say them out loud for extra impact.

5. For best results, record them over your favorite tunes.

Dream Building Examples

Here's a few examples (without the photos).

I have **Composed** some of the coolest tunes on the planet! Achieved on:
I've **Donated** instruments to those less fortunate than myself, so they too can experience the joy of music. Achieved on:
I enjoy the **Finest Things** life has to offer! Family, friends, happiness, music, love, health, and plenty of financial resources. Achieved on:
I am an individual who has reached my **Full-Potential**. Achieved on:
I own an impressive **Guitar Collection.** I love playing my acoustic and electric guitars daily! Achieved on:
I have a **Harmonious Life** because I built it on a solid foundation. Achieved on:
I own a nice **Home** in a quiet neighbourhood. It suits my lifestyle perfectly! Achieved on:
I own a nice **Light Show**, the band looks great onstage! Achieved on:
I enjoy making a **Living** helping others achieve their dreams! Achieved on:
I own a nice **Speaker System.** I'm amazed at how great it sounds every time I crank it up! Achieved on:
I own a **Trailer** to get my rig around town. It suits my needs perfectly! Achieved on:
I own a dependable **Vehicle** that gets the band around in comfort! Achieved on:

Congratulations On Working Up Your Customized Dream List!

So How Many Did You End Up With?

Notes And Thoughts

Notes And Thoughts

Workshop 4 Fun With Building A Rig And Playlist

In this workshop, I will offer some suggestions on putting together a rig and playlist. After working up my three mindset fundamentals, it was time for me to put together a great sounding speaker system and a playlist of tunes I wanted to perform. I created three lists. The first was a list of tunes I thought I could perform well and enjoyed playing. The second list was gear I currently owned. The third list was gear I needed to acquire to complete my set up.

Next, I sketched out some ideas of what my rig was going to look like and then started looking around for used gear because I had limited financial resources. My rig had to be dependable, sound great and could be set up within an hour... so I kept that in mind when piecing it together.

Once I purchased the gear needed, I created a load up checklist so nothing would be left behind. I also made an inventory list of what was going to be covered on an insurance policy in case I ever got cleaned out leaving my rig in a bar or nightclub over the weekend. After about a month of learning tunes and piecing together my rig, it was exciting to know that I was pretty much ready to start looking for gigs!

If you have a great sounding rig and get your tunes down, it will help you keep gigs in the books!

Workshop Instructions:

1. Make a list of tunes you would like to play at your gigs.

2. Make a list of what gear you own and need.

3. Sketch out an example of what your rig will look like.

4. Piece together your rig (mixer, speakers, lights etc.) as soon as possible.

5. Inventory everything including cables, connectors, accessories etc. for an insurance policy.

6. Shop around and acquire an insurance policy that offers the best rates and coverage.

7. Make a load up checklist so you always have what you need at the gig.

8. Inventory your home studio gear/instruments and add it to the policy as well. Covering your keister is the most important thing you can do today!

Rig And Playlist Suggestions

Annual Maintenance- If you take care of your gear, your gear will take care of you. Every year give everything a nice cleaning along with spraying the contacts with deoxIT D5 contact cleaner. Your equipment should last for years if you take care of it.

Back Up Gear- Bringing backup gear to a gig is highly recommended. Having a back up speaker, sub, power amp, mixer, power supplies, laptop...etc. is a great idea! You're in the rock n roll business... there's going to be rock n roll casualties so be prepared. I had a power amp melt down at a gig and had my replacement hooked up within a few minutes. It saved me big time!

Build Your Rig To Impress- Make sure your rig looks and sounds impressive. That's one way to get the call back!

Cables- If possible, buy patch and xlr cables that offer a lifetime warranty. I recommend Livewire, Monster and Mogami cables.

Cases- I love SKB cases and recommend them. All SKB cases come with a lifetime warranty and I have used them for 30 years.

Circuit Tester- Plugging in a circuit tester before using any wall outlet is highly recommended. It will keep you out of trouble. Don't fry your gear because someone wired it incorrectly. I have run across a few improperly wired outlets over the years so please do this every time.

DJ Station- I converted a two-tier keyboard stand into a DJ station and it works great! I put a couple of laptops on it, a mini mixer and song lists on the top tier.

DMX Cables- There are great deals on DMX cables at amazon.com.

Drum Mics- If you cannot afford hi-end drum mics, Digital Reference drum mics work well and are economical.

Effects Processors- I love T.C Electronics, Roland, MXR, Fulltone and recommend them.

Fog Machine- Customers love it, I recommend it if the venue allows it! You can buy a mini fogger for around fifty bucks.

Guitars- I love all guitars that stay in tune... acoustics and electrics. Superstrats with a floyd are my personal favorites. People love acoustic and electric guitars so I recommend bringing both to the gig. Please let your stagehand know that your guitars are FRAGILE and need to be handled with care. They should be the last thing put on the stage after setting up and the first thing taken off the stage and put in cases when the show is over.

Guitar Amps- I love the Roland Jazz Chorus JC-120 for clean tones and a Marshall JCM 800 for the distorted tones. For practical reasons, I only take the Marshall out to gigs. High gain tube amps sound great to me and recommend them. Consider putting plexiglass in front of your speaker cabinet so you don't drive the soundman crazy and kill the person standing 30 feet away directly in the line of fire.

Hand Trucks- I recommend the RocknRoller Multi-Cart. I own the R10 and R12 model. They are amazing and has served our band for decades.

Hum Eliminator- I recommend getting a Rolls HE18 Hum Eliminator for your 'Buzz Off' needs. It has saved me a few times when there are ground loop challenges in a venue.

Inflatable's- Customers love inflatable instruments and I like to have some of them available as gifts! If you want to see someone come out of their shell, throw out some inflatable's! You can purchase them online at Rhode Island Novelty.

Insuring Your Gear- As covered earlier, insuring your gear is a wise thing to do. I've heard too many horror stories over the years of gear/instruments getting stolen. Simply inventory all your gear, simply put a replacement value on it and get a policy with an e-z pay program. C.Y.A. Today!

Labels- I recommend labeling all your gear/cables so everyone knows who it belongs to.

Laptops- I recommend going to craigslist and checking out economical laptops so you can hopefully get two of them. Having an on-demand backup ready to dial in at any second is vital. Laptops are fragile so make sure you put them in your vehicle for a softer ride to and from gigs.

Load In And Load Out- I recommend working up a load in and load out system to maximize speed and efficiency. On band gigs, I give myself 3 to 4 hours to set up and two hours for tearing it down. On DJ gigs, I give myself 1.5 hours to set up and an hour to tear down.

Microphones For Vocals- I recommend Shure SM 58's and Sennhieser G3 wireless mics. They sound great!

Monitors For Vocals- I use and recommend the Mackie 15" Thump powered speakers.

Mixers- I've used Mackie mixers for years and love them. I currently use and recommend the Behringer X-18 digital mixers.

Playlist Selection- I recommend learning a variety of tunes to appeal to the widest range of customers. Visit djintelligence.com for tune selection ideas.

Power Amps- I love Crown amps and recommend them.

Power Conditioners- I've had great success with Furman power conditioners and recommend them.

Rig Appearance- Impressive should be the word that comes to mind when customers look at your rig. Do not cut corners when putting it together.

Safety First! Always take measures to ensure the safety of everyone moving gear around.

Scrolling Sign- Customers love to see their name in lights so consider getting a scrolling sign for your events.

Security- Everyone should know there are professional thieves everywhere and they are watching you! Avoid being easy prey. Don't leave your gear unattended, or out in your vehicle overnight. The best (or blast) advice I can give you is to take extra steps by making it hard for thieves to steal anything you own. Make them want to move on to easier targets.

Speakers- I love RCF Speakers driven with Crown amps! What a combo! I have been using this setup for years and I'm still amazed on how great they sound! I recommend going to a music store like Guitar Center and hearing all the different kinds of speakers available so you will know what you like. I'm really impressed with the QSC powered speakers and the BOSE systems. By the way, if you are low on dough, there's nothing wrong with buying used gear...half of retail is usually the going rate. The mid-hi speakers I use are 400 watts each and are pushed by a Crown amp 660 watts per side. It's perfect for small and mid-sized events. On larger gigs, I add the subs that are 800 watts per side being pushed by a Crown amp 1200 watt a side. Having a great sounding speaker system will help you in getting the call back!

Stage Area Lighting- I use the Chauvet Tri-Bar, Chauvet 4 Play CL and the American DJ Vertigo. They create a nice ambience and are easy to set up/tear down. I also use two min lasers to point at the ceiling and use two Chauvet SlimPar 56 for up lighting. Customers will appreciate any lighting and effects you bring to the gig!

Stagehands- Stagehands should be trained properly before their first gig. Work up a set up/tear down system, type it up and email it to them. The more detailed, the better. This will ensure a smooth-running show.

Tune Building- Make a list tunes you love and would consider performing at your gigs. Create a doc and copy/paste the lyrics. Next, grab the YouTube link of the original and karaoke version and paste it on your doc. Practice it until it is smooth as silk.

Tune Learning Techniques - The best way I have found to learn tunes is to slap the lyrics on a doc, set up the arrangement, fly in the chords, check out what the bass player is doing, learn the rhythm guitar parts and then learn the leads so I have a good overall picture of how the tune is constructed. If you practice the tunes in your head and visualize the chart you made up, it will help you remember everything a little easier.

Tune Research- If you plan on booking weddings and corporate events, you will want to learn a variety of tunes. Check out djintelligence.com for a list of the overall top 200 songs requested. It's a great resource to see what is currently trending as well.

Congratulations On Putting Together Your Rig And Playlist!

Notes And Thoughts

Notes And Thoughts

Workshop 5 Fun With Scripts

In this workshop I will show you how to work up some scripts for effective communication. Being that I had just built up a rig and practiced my butt off learning tunes, it was time for me to start looking for gigs. I wasn't sure what to say to restaurant and club owners except that I have a one-man band show and would like to play at their place.

After making a bunch of telephone calls, I decided to create some scripts to guide me through the process of convincing someone to hire me. It didn't take long for me to figure out that conveying the right message at the right time means booking more gigs.

Here's the top scripts I currently use most often and recommend everyone create some of their own. Meeting someone on an elevator, leaving a voicemail, sending an email, making follow up calls, emailing presentations or filling out a hot lead sheet... should all be scripted to stay on point. They will work to your advantage if you take the time to create some for your needs.

You could very well turn out to be one of the world's most effective communicators simply by creating scripts. One things for sure, you'll book and perform more gigs because of it!

Workshop Instructions:

1. Review the following eight scripts.

2. Create your own version of each and start using them right away.

3. Work up others as needed to keep your communications efficient and effective.

Script 1 Elevator Speech

An elevator script is simply giving someone you just met a quick rundown on who you are, what you do, how you serve and why you love doing what you do.

Practice your elevator script until it rolls off your tongue like honey. It should not be any longer than 20 seconds.

Here's a few examples:

"Hello, my name is Rick, we have a music service in town offering live bands, djs, and karaoke. We love making people happy through the magic of music, here's my card!"

"Hello, my name is Rick, I teach musicians how to book and perform gigs by sharing our unique success formulas we've developed over the years. I love teaching it because every musician deserves a nice paying gig!"

Script 2 Initial Email To A Potential Customer Who Is Inquiring About Your Services

Subject Line

Good Morning/Afternoon [Customer Name], Have The Best [Event Type] Ever With [Your Product Or Service]!

Body

We Have Several Talent Options Available So Give Us A Shout At [Your Phone Number]!

Helping Customers Celebrate Life's Special Moments With Family, Friends And Co-workers

Is Our Specialty! Your Satisfaction Is Always Guaranteed!

Check Out Our Celebration Page: [Your Link To Videos, Pictures, Talent And Reviews]

Outstanding Reasons To Hire [Your Product Or Service] For Your Special Event:

*You'll Look Like A Party Planning Genius!
*[Your Product Or Service] Has Been Trusted By [Some Of Your Customers]!
*You'll Get A High Energy, Non-Stop Party At Reasonable Rates!
*You Get The Finest Quality!
*Huge Live Song List!
*You Get To Customize Your Event! (Give Them A Few Talent Options)

*You Will Hear A Great Sounding Speaker System!

*You'll Get Some Stage Area Lighting! You'll Look Marvelous Dancing The Night Away!

*You'll Get A Group Picture To Share & Cherish Forever!

*Peace Of Mind! You Can Forget About Falling Victim To A Lame Party!

There's Limited Availability On Our Services And It's First Come First Served So To Avoid Being Disappointed, Give Us A Call Today!

Thanks For Your Consideration,

[Your Name, Phone Number And Website]

[Any Recent Publicity You Have Received]

Here's What A Few Of Our Happy Customers Are Saying:

[Add A Few Customer Reviews/Testimonials]

Script 3 Follow Up Phone Call

"Good Morning/Evening [Customer's Name], this is [Your Name] with [Your Company]. I'm checking in with you to see if we could be of service to you on [Date Of Event]. I sent you an email outlining a bunch of cool things we can offer you on the big day! Please give us a shout before making a buying decision; we would like the opportunity to earn your business! My cell is [Your Phone Number]... that's [Your Phone Number]. If you want to have a perfect [Type Of Event], please reach out to me... I'll be right here waiting on your call...thank you [Customer's Name]."

Script 4 Follow Up Email

"Hello [Customer's Name], is our name still in the hat for your [Type Of Event] on [Date Of Event]? We are here to serve!" Optional: "I have some discounts for you if you care to give me a call!"

Script 5 A Fond Farewell Email

(Use this on your seventh and final attempt to work with a potential customer. It's simply a last-ditch effort to earn their business and it works sometimes because people want what they cannot have.

Subject: A Fond Farewell From [Your Name].

Body
We feel bad that you will not be using our services because we were looking forward to working with your organization. Thanks for your consideration anyway.

Keep us on file as a plan 'B' if plan 'A' does not work out!
Could you please tell us where we went off track?
Was it price or quality?

Please let us know if we could improve our presentation... we always want to know what customers think about our promotional materials.

Also, please pass along our company info to someone we could be of service to.

We do pay referral fees and would like the opportunity to send you some cash!

Best wishes to you, [Your Name, Number And Web Site]

Script 6 Prospecting Phone Call

"Hello, my name is [Your Name], we have a music service in town that offers live bands, djs and karaoke! I'm calling today to see if we could be of service to you and if so, wanted to email over some info on us!"

If they are not interested say, "Do you know of anyone who might be interested in using our services? We do offer cash referral fees!"

Script 7 Thank You Email (Email this within 24 hours of the gig.)

Subject Line

Hi [Customer Name]! Thanks for using our services! Here are your party photos/video!

Body

Thank you for allowing us to be of service to you last night.

Nice job on putting together a cool [Type Of Event].

We love to get comments from customers; do you have any kind words for us to share with folks inquiring about our services?

If so, simply reply back to us or click the following link and leave a review.

By the way, we do offer cash referral fees so please recommend us to anyone looking for a band, dj or karaoke for their special event!

Here's the sharable link to the party photos/video: [Link]

Take care, thanks for your business, and we hope to work with you again soon!

[Your Name]

Script 8 Hot Lead Sheet

The hot lead script is six questions and one comment embedded in the form on the following page. Simply use these as you work your way through the conversation with your customer taking notes as you go.

Here's what the acronyms mean:

toe= type of event, wp? =weather permitting, doe=date of event, loe=location of event, hoe=hours of event and aoe=attendance of event. I recommend creating your own version of the hot lead sheet and put several in a binder for quick reference or create an online version of it so you capture event details quickly when customers call.

DATE_____ [ ] 1. Used us before? [ ] 2. May I take some notes?
3. [ ] Can you tell me all about the perfect [Type Of Entertainment]?_____
4. [ ] Sounds to me like we'd fit in perfectly with the festivities!

EVENT#_____

EVENT WISHES & DESIRES (Hot Buttons)_____ Surprise? Y N

Hot Lead= Stay Close To The Customer

NAME_____ COMPANY_____

PHONE(s)_____

EMAIL_____

Need a :

BAND_____ DJ_____ KJ_____ Musician_____ Videographer_____ Audio Visual_____ Other_____

TOE_____ WP?___ DOE_____ Mon Tue Wed Thu Fri Sat Sun AM PM

LOE_____ HOE_____ AOE_____ SET UP BY___

5. [ ] What's the most you want to invest on the music part?

Outside: Y N Cover: Y N Weather: Y N Attire_____ **Price Range$**_____

STAIRS?_____ ELECRICITY/FT_____ STAGE/FT./FLOOR_____ PARKING VALIDATION? Y N

TALENT RECOMMENDED_____ PHONE_____ Email_____

SERVICE FEE AGREED TO_____ SENT FROM_____

ACTIVITY_____
_____

MARKETING SOURCE: Repeat_____ WOM_____ Internet_____ Search Engine_____

Keywords_____ Other_____

Post Gig: THANK YOU ___email sent___pic___vid___venue___social fb___blog___youtube___

6.[ ] Will you **promise** to call me back <u>before</u> deciding to at least give us the opportunity to work with you?
     Will you **promise**?
7.[ ] Any more questions?
Slash it?=First time/existing/military/law enforcement/vip discount?
Additional notes:

Notes And Thoughts

Notes And Thoughts

Workshop 6 Fun With Prospecting And Marketing

In this workshop I will teach you how to be a prospecting and marketing expert. After playing in restaurants and clubs for a while, I decided to up my game and start doing better paying gigs like weddings and company parties. Customers at my gigs were inquiring about my services for these types of events but I didn't know about the ins and outs of doing them.

I knew that the checks were going to be bigger in that market so agreed to do a few weddings and corporate events to see what they were all about. I ended up loving private sector gigs and wanted to do more of them and that brings us to the very important topic of prospecting and marketing. It's something you must get good at if you want the great paying gigs.

Prospecting and marketing is the lifeblood to any business. It's something that should be worked on a few hours each day. Getting the right message in front of the right person at the right time so they request more information is the name of the game for continued success in booking and performing nice paying gigs.

The combination of outbound calls/emails and investing up to 10% of your gross revenue towards effective marketing should create enough high-quality leads for you to be successful at booking gigs simply by playing the numbers game.

You just might end up having a bunch of decent paying gigs in the books because of your prospecting and marketing efforts!

Workshop Instructions:

1. Review the marketing and prospecting strategies.

2. Review the prospecting sources list and create one for your prospecting efforts.

3. Review the goal implementation graph and create one so you can keep track of your outbound calls and emails.

4. Start dialing for dollars using the scripts you created in workshop 4.

Prospecting And Marketing Strategies

Business Booster- The best way to get the phone ringing is to start making outbound calls. If business gets slow, start dialing for dollars and sending out emails.

Business Cards- Sign up with Vistaprint and create some cool looking business cards. Order a bunch of them and hand them out to everyone! Make sure you put a coupon on the back and a few testimonials.

Community Outreach- Make a habit of reaching out to the community via phone calls and emails at least one hour a day (preferably in the morning) and document your activity on your goal implementation graph. The energy you put forth in the marketplace will always come back to you in some form or fashion.

Email/Call Sequence- When going down your hot leads, alternate between calls and emails. Potential customers will appreciate your follow up and often will hire you just because you were persistent.

Email Subject Line- Change up your subject lines and use their name on each email to prevent customers from tuning you out. They are bombarded with emails and this will help you get their attention.

Entertainment Agencies- Agencies can be great resources for gigs if you lucky enough to get their attention. Reach out to them and let them know that you would like to be of service to them and their customers. Send an email to them periodically with a link to your agent friendly site (one that does not have your contact information displayed). A great way to get them to work with you is to send them some customers if you are already booked.

Family And Friends- We all love our family and friends but if you let them, they will eat up your business day. Set a time limit on phone calls from family and friends to five minutes max during business hours and offer to call them back later. If a friend wants to drop by during business hours, tell them that you will put them to work. Some of them just might drop by and help hunt down gigs.

Flyers- Create some flyers and start posting them all over the place. Folks will see them and call you. This marketing strategy is perfect if you are low on funds and need to get the word out fast!

Follow Up Strategy- Stay close to the customer on all hot leads. A phone call, email or text is appropriate to keep from getting lost in the shuffle. Reach out to hot leads often to increase your chances of getting the gig. Every other day is good for a few emails and then once a week.

Goal Implementation Graph- I created the goal implementation graph, as shown at the end of this workshop, to keep track of how many outbound calls/emails I was making. It's a great tool to use in keeping your head in the game. I recommend you create one for your prospecting efforts as well. At the end of each month, add up the weekly totals so you will know how well you are doing at playing the numbers game.

Hot Lead Follow Up- Working the incoming hot leads from potential customers will eventually generate gigs. Copy and paste all your leads coming in from the internet on a doc for easy follow up tracking.

Hot Lead Urgency- When you get a hot lead, email your promo out quickly and give them an initial phone call to introduce yourself. One minute can change a gig opportunity.

Marketing Mojo- We are not in the music business; we are in the marketing business. Be an expert by continuously studying the subject and stay aggressive with your marketing campaigns.

Marketing Strategies- I recommend having at least three effective marketing strategies going at once. There's strength in diversity so keep experimenting with different marketing sources and decide which work best.

Marketing Tracking- Ask potential customers how they found out about you to track your marketing efforts. Review your results monthly and decide where your dollars are best invested.

Networking With Entertainment Agents - Agents are great to work with! Entertainment Agents should be a part of your success formula if you are lucky enough to get their attention. They have invested years in building relationships with their customer base and should be compensated well for their expertise.

Networking With Musicians- Offer every musician you meet a cash referral fee if they hook you up with a gig.

Online Memberships- Gigmasters, Gigsalad, and Punchbowl are just a few online sites that could produce quality gigs for you. Try them out for a while and see.

Prospecting Formula- Successful prospecting is simply playing the numbers game. The more calls and emails you make, the more opportunities you will generate. Some folks will like what you have to offer, some won't. Simply share with them what you do in the best light possible and let them decide if they want to do business with you.

Prospecting Fun- Make prospecting fun by not thinking of it as work. Think of it as making new friends! Put on your favorite music, at a low volume, when you're prospecting to keep yourself in a good mood and enthusiasm level up. Potential customers will pick up on the fact that you enjoy what you are doing. If they like you, they will buy from you... it doesn't matter what you are selling or for how much! Get them laughing and having a good time right away to get a good shot at earning their business.

Prospecting And Marketing Formula- Spend one hour each on marketing and prospecting every day to generate consistent opportunities in the marketplace. Opportunity is always!

Prospecting Habits- I've found that sixty minute prospecting sessions followed by a ten minute walk around break works best in avoiding fatigue. I also recommend using full-spectrum lighting at your desk and of course a comfortable chair that promotes good posture. Also keep a mirror on your desk as a reminder for you to smile a lot when speaking with customers. Smiles can be heard!

Prospecting Hours- Anytime during business hours is fine when prospecting but the sweet spot is between 9:30am and 11:30 am. Studies have shown that you are more likely to catch someone at their desk during these times. I've also found that Saturday mornings are a great time to make follow up calls.

Quarterly Emails To Existing Customers- Create a short sweet and to the point script and email it to your existing customers every three months. Perhaps offer some existing customer discounts or weekly specials to motivate them to hire you for a gig.

Referrals- As always, let everyone know that you pay cash referral fees if they hook you up with a gig.

Social Media- Create a social media presence so folks can follow you. YouTube and Facebook are a must.

Successful Selling Facts- Reach out to 100 contacts and expect several of them to turn into customers!

Vocal Presentations- Your voice can make a big impact on your ability to convince and convey. Use your voice like a musical instrument playing a song. Add varying pitch, volume, and length of sound. Speak with zest and zeal like you are having the best day of your life! It will keep the listener interested. As far as breathing technique and posture, breathe through your nose so you don't dry out your vocal cords, sit up straight (if you are sitting down) and keep your shoulders back. Also drink plenty of water so you do not get dehydrated. When you speak, you are losing moisture.

Website Power- You only have a few seconds to capture a potential customer's attention so make your website captivating, fun and interactive. Customers love stories so give them lots of customer reviews along with videos, photo galleries, faq's, song lists, event planners, etc. Give them reasons why they should do business with you and have your contact info on every page. Invest a little time and do some research to see what everyone else is doing then design yours. In my opinion, a great website answers every question a potential customer might have, except for how much (that's where the phone call comes in)... so start building your website today!

Now that we have gone over some prospecting and marketing strategies, I will show you where to get the gigs.

Prospecting Sources

Here's a list of places to get gigs. There is opportunity everywhere so pick out some categories and simply start dialing for dollars. Do an internet search in your city to find out who to contact. Asking for permission to email them some information is common courtesy.

If you are working from an alphabetical list, start in the Z's and work your way up to the A's! The folks in the Z's are dying to get phone calls!

Create a goal implementation graph like the one on the next page to track your efforts by knowing how many calls, emails and texts you have made. The energy you put forth in the marketplace will always come back at you in some form or fashion.

American Legions
Art Galleries
Auto Dealerships
Band Managers
Banks
Beach Clubs
Bowling Alleys
Bridal Shows
Caterers
Chamber Of Commerce
Churches
City Concert Series
City Coronations
Civic Centers
Colleges
Corporations

Country Clubs
County Fairs
County Parks
Entertainment Agencies
Event Planners
Existing Customers
Festivals
Fortune 500 Companies
Google (local, seo and pay per click)
Graduation Parties
Grand Openings
Government Agencies
Homeowners Associations
Hotels
Industrial Parks
Malls
Marinas
Moose Lodge
Movie Theaters
Museums
Musician Networking
Neighborhoods
New Year's Eve Celebrations
Night Clubs
Political Parties
Private Clubs
Private Parties
Pool Parties
Proms
Resorts
Restaurants
Retirement Communities
Schools

Seasonal Events
Shopping Centers
Small Businesses
Social Clubs
Social Media
Special Event Facilities
Subdivisions
Trade Shows
Universities
Vendors You Meet At Gigs
Wedding Planners

The harder you work, the luckier you get so have fun reaching out to the community!

Play the numbers game and deserve victory! Keep track of your daily prospecting sessions (calls, emails and texts) with this document!

Have A Blast Booking And Performing Gigs

"It's Fun Reaching Out To The Community!"   "It's Fun Being Successful!"   Month_____

Goal Implementation Graph

Mon.	Tues.	Wed.	Thurs.	Fri.	Sat.	Sun.
Date						Weekly totals and notes
Date						
Date						
Date						
Date						

Existing	Agents	Bands/DJs	Clubs	SEF/Vendors	Managers	Misc.

I've booked_____   I've networked_____   YTD Gigs Book_____

Notes And Thoughts

Notes And Thoughts

Workshop 7 Fun With Being An Expert Advisor

In this workshop, I will show you how to be an expert fun advisor. Low pressure selling is the best way to book gigs. If you are treating potential customers like an old friend, they will lower their defenses.

This makes selling your services much easier. Customers also like options so I always offer a few so that they can decide what best suits their needs.

Practicing the art and science of drawing out hot buttons, offering options/solutions that make sense to them and having some decent emotionally driven promo should allow you to earn your fair share of the multi-billion-dollar entertainment pie.

You could very well have a calendar full of great paying gigs because you took the time to learn the following strategies.

Workshop Instructions:

1. Review and practice the following fun advisor strategies.

2. Try them out with potential customers.

3. Be on the lookout for more of them, you will find new ones along the way.

Expert Fun Advisor Strategies

Affirmations – Great advisors will have a warm up session by going over some sales related affirmations 15 minutes before they make their first call or email.

Appearance When Visiting Folks- Expert fun advisors know the importance of looking their best when visiting with potential customers. Nice dress shoes, slacks and a buttoned shirt or polo is perfect!

Art of Asking- As covered earlier, when a potential customer contacts you, ask if they have used your services before. It makes it seem like your company has served so many people over the years.

Art of Asking- Ask for the gig when you feel the time is right. Simply say, "Would you like for me to go ahead and fill out an agreement, so you can take this off your to do list?"

Art of Asking- If you are turned down for a gig ask, "Was it because of price or quality that made you go with someone else?" This will shed light on how things went down and can help you adjust your marketing strategies.

Art of Asking- Great advisors ask, "When's a good time to check back in with you?"

Art of Asking- Ask the customer to give you some feedback and/or put a grade on your presentation. Customer feedback will help you strengthen your promo.

Art of Asking- Ask your customer, "What's the biggest frustration you are having looking for a [Type Of Entertainment]?" This is a great question and will help you in market positioning.

Art of Asking– Ask your customer, "Is there anything we can do to earn your business today? We are here to serve!"

Art of Asking- Say this to your customer when they ask you what your quote is, "What does my quote need to be to earn your business? I'm sure you're getting quotes all over the map right? What's the most you want to invest on the music part of your [Type Of Event]?

Benefits Selling- Communicate the benefits of doing business with you often with your potential customers! Run down a list of all the cool things they will be getting. Say something like, "By placing your buying decision with us, you'll get expert talent, a great sounding speaker system, lights; tons of fun music along with our satisfaction guarantee... you'll look like a party planning genius! Would that make you happy?"

Business Cards- Great advisors have plenty of business cards and hand them out to everyone they can!

Buying Decision Comment- Congratulate your customers on making a wise buying decision when they hire you! It makes them feel good and helps eliminate any buyer remorse they may have.

Competitive Spirit- Great advisors have a friendly competitive spirit without slandering anyone. It is not good business to slander anyone so avoid doing it.

Committee Selling- If a potential customer tells you that they are sharing your information with a committee, offer to bring them a gift if they figure out a way to put you over the top.

Committee Selling- Offer to drop by and meet the committee!

Congratulations- Congratulate your customer when you are done negotiating with them by saying, "Congratulations, brilliant job negotiating!" It makes them feel good that they are doing business with you!

Concessions- If a potential customer is asking for a concession (discount or something extra thrown in), simply say, "If I can make that happen, would you be willing to make a buying decision today?"

Considerations- A lot of potential customers are advisors/salespeople themselves and appreciate a well thought out sales presentation... they will hire you simply for that reason alone.

Convincing Powers – Convincing customers with emotionally driven presentations (videos, pictures, customer reviews) and conveying value is smart selling.

Customer Concerns- If a customer raises an area of concern say, "I understand, a few of our customers also felt the same way...but after using our services they found that it was not an issue. Do you have any other areas of concern?"

Customers Favorite Word- The customer's favorite word is their name so use it often but do not over use it.

Customer Information Gathering- Great advisors ask a lot of questions to capture the customers desires quickly.

Customer Service- Great advisors stay close to their customers. An initial email and call should be customary as well as a robust follow-up system.

Customer Service- Great advisors strive to offer the best customer service available anywhere! Be quick in your replies to them if they call or email you.

Customer Comfort- Customers are going to buy from the person that makes them feel most comfortable. As covered earlier, treat them like an old friend, their defenses will drop, and they will open up to you.

Customer Spotlight- A great advisor puts the spotlight on the customer and not on themselves.

Deposit Received Courtesy Call Or Email- Give customers a courtesy call or email when their initial investment/deposit has arrived.

Discounts- Great advisors offer discounts to first time customers as well as existing customers. Everyone loves discounts! Say something like, "I'll slash 20% off today to earn your business… will that work for you?"

Discounts That Are Time Sensitive – Offer a weekly sale something like 20% Off This Week Only! If the offer expires and a potential customer asks about it, offer to extend the discount for a limited time to entice them to go ahead and make a buying decision!

Distractions- Great advisors are never in a hurry and take extra steps to give customers their undivided attention. Avoid multitasking when working with customers.

Ego- Putting the customer's ego first before your own is the mark of a great expert fun advisor.

Email Speediness- Email your presentation to a potential customer right away to hopefully get them emotionally involved. I recommend attaching your customer reviews as well so they can see the level of quality you bring to the table.

Empathizing- Put yourself in their shoes and tell them that you understand where they are coming from... then offer solutions.

Etiquette- Always let customers end their sentences...and allow them to interrupt yours if they so desire.

Follow Up- There's fortune in follow up! Reach out to potential customers at least 6 times before sending out a fond farewell email.

Friendly Words- Use soft, friendly words when speaking to your customers, you'll get much better results:

Instead of using the word **appointment**, use **visit**.

Instead of using the word **budget**, use the words **investment range**.

Instead of using the word **cheaper**, use **more economical**.

Instead of using the word **client**, use **the special customers we serve**.

Instead of using the words **closing the sale**, use **consummating the transaction**.

Instead of using the word **commission**, use **service fee or fee for service**.

Instead of using the word **contract**, use **agreement**.

Instead of using the word **problem**, use **area of concern or challenges**.

Instead of using the word **sign here**, use **authorize, approve, sign off or okay the paperwork**.

Gifts And Giveaways- Great advisors offer gifts and giveaways to customers regularly because they know the power of reciprocity. Offer gifts to customers just for calling you up, at gigs when you arrive or anytime.

Hot Buttons- Great advisors know how to draw out hot buttons by asking the right questions and then putting them into their presentation. Customers will spill the beans if you ask them to. There's usually one or two main objectives they have in mind for their event so simply ask them what they are.

Heart First Selling Second- Be a potential customer's friend first and let them know you care about them and the success of their special event. Customers love having their heart strings pulled and you should have no problem booking a lot of gigs if you pull them!

Investment Scale Selling- As an expert fun advisor it's important to know your marketplace so you can find out from a potential customer where they are on the investment scale. This will help you recommend the right talent for their needs. You can say something like, "High end top of the market bands are [Price] and you can get a low-quality band for around [Price]. Then ask, where along the scale would you like to be?"

Learning Curves- Customers need a little time to look over the presentation you emailed them. Give them a little time to review the information and then call them to see if they have any questions for you.

Low Budgets- If you have a potential customer that wants you to be a cheap date simply say, "That's not a realistic rate for an expert... is there any creative way to get your numbers up?"

Magic Numbers- Sometimes customers will reveal right up front what their magic number is. Simply decide if it's a number you can work with. If it is, fill out a special event agreement right away.

Missed Gigs- If you miss out on a gig, put the potential customers email on your quarterly list. Perhaps you can be of service to them in the future.

Objection Handling – Practice these three steps on any objections you might get from customers. 1. Agree with them (I can understand you feeling that way...) 2. Call them by name (Well John and Mary....) 3. Ask them a question (If we could fix that situation, would that make you happy?)

Objection Reply - When a potential customer has an objection about anything, say "There's obviously a reason why you brought that up... would you please share that with me?"

Options – As covered earlier, customers love choices so give them a few but not more than three. Here's one I like to use, "Would you like to add our female singers, horn section or both to the talent line-up?"

Over The Years Statement- Advising from experience is a wise move. "Over the years, we've found that there's always one or two main reasons why folks hire our band... what might those reasons be for you?"

Paperwork- Great advisors use easy to fill out paperwork and documents. Customers love easy!

Passion Selling- Great advisors are passionate and really believe in what they are selling.

Persuasion Selling Statement- Say something like this, "If we help you have the perfect wedding day, a lifetime of wonderful memories and make you look like a party planning genius, would [Your Quote] be a fair rate to ask for?".

Phone Etiquette- If you're on the phone with a potential customer and you get another call coming in, let it go to voicemail. Customers deserve your undivided attention.

Plan B- Expert advisors always have a plan B ready to go if plan A does not work out! Maybe your potential customer do not have the financial resources for a full band so offer some alternate talent options like a duo, single or DJ.

Planning Mojo- Great advisors are great planners! Plan out your schedule hourly, daily, weekly and monthly. You will get much more done and keep your brain engaged on the tasks at hand.

Positioning- Great advisors are interested extroverts rather than interesting introverts. Put the spotlight on the customer and you will have a much greater chance of booking a gig.

Prayer Power- Great advisors do a lot of praying and never give up no matter what!

Presentation Length- Make your presentations short sweet and to the point, use a lot of videos and communicate the benefits. You can always offer them more information if they ask for it.

Presentation Energy- The more energy you put in your presentation, the less you will have to exert when the customer is ready to make a buying decision.

Price Juxtaposition- Always compare your services to a higher priced service. Customers love value so create it for them by justifying what you are asking.

Pros & Cons- Ben Franklin made a lot of decisions by creating a list of pros and cons on a sheet of paper. Try it out, it works! Get out a sheet of paper; draw a line down the middle of it. Write down all the pros of doing something on the left side and the cons on the right side. Base your decision on which ever column is longer. This also works with customers... you can give them all the pros of doing business with you...and then let them fill in the cons by themselves if they can think of any.

Quarterly Contacts- Great advisors keep a database of existing customers and reach out to them quarterly.

Rapport- Building a close and harmonious relationship with a potential customer quickly will greatly increase your chances of doing business with them. Find something they like and talk about that for a minute or two... it works wonders!

Research- Google your potential customer, learn their love language and start using it.

Rejection Handling- Being turned down for a gig shouldn't be taken personally. Maybe they are not ready for your service right now. Put them on your quarterly list. Let rejection roll off your back.

Sales Crash- Lose a gig? Forget about it! It happens to all great advisors. Shake it off and look forward to serving today's new customers.

Sales Mastery- Benjamin Franklin once said, "Tell me and I forget, teach me and I may remember, involve me and I learn". In other words, involve your potential customers quickly with song lists and planners to emotionally hook them.

Let's twist that quote into this, "Tell me and I might remember, show me and I'll probably forget... involve me and I'll understand".

Satisfaction Guarantee- Always offer a satisfaction guarantee. Customers do expect it.

Scarcity Statements- Great advisors know the power of scarcity and always put some of these kinds of statements in their presentations. Here are a few examples. We have one left! Discount ends at midnight! Don't snooze and lose! Key dates fill up quickly so to avoid being disappointed, call us today! Based on the number of inquiries we've been getting, that date won't last very long!

Selling Formula- Selling is 95% psychology and 5% math. Work on the psychology part of your presentation and the rest of the formula will work out.

Sizzle Selling- Great advisors know that they are 'selling the sizzle, and not the steak' on their products and services.

Special Reports- Special reports are really sales letters in disguise. Work one up and include it with your presentation.

Speed Matching- Some customers talk fast while others speak slowly. Match their speed so you do not create a disconnect. You can slowly adjust the speed as the conversation progresses but start off where they are.

Statements That Work- When you feel the time is right say, "May we earn your business today?".

Statements That Work- "Everyone on our team will take such great care of you!"

Stress Dropper For Customers – Sharing testimonials and stories of some of the events you have been doing will lower your potential customer's stress level.

Stress Dropper For You- Practice makes perfect! The more you practice the better you get which will raise your confidence level. Practice these strategies daily to keep your stress level down.

Superstar Selling Statement- When a potential customer wants to know about the booking process say this, "It's easy doing business with us… whenever you're ready to make a buying decision, we'll fill out an agreement and email it over to you… sign it and send it in with the deposit and we are all set… it's that easy!".

Teaming Up- Great advisors will team up with their customers instead of taking an opposing view. Team up with them on their top 3 objectives!

Thank You- Say 'thank you' a lot. Customers love and appreciate it!

Throw In Extra Stuff- Great advisors throw stuff in for free! Free Karaoke! Free DJ! Free Upgrade!

Visiting With Potential Customers- If a potential customer wants to meet in person, let them decide when and where. Always arrive 10 minutes early and bring them a gift of some sort. Have your hot lead sheet on a clipboard so you can take additional notes and have them look over the event planners. Do show them you customer reviews and some photos on your tablet or phone if they have not already seen them. Do offer to fill out an agreement right then and there…and get a deposit. Have an extra pen handy as well just in case the one you are using gives out.

What Put You Over The Top Question- When a customer decides to book you for their event, ask them what put you over the top. It will shed light on what you are doing correctly.

Why Customers Use Our Services Statement- Come up with a great line as to why customers would want to do business with you. You can say something like, "Most customers use us because we offer the finest quality, great service and value around!".

Words And Phrases To Avoid- Great advisors avoid the words 'honestly', "I'll be honest with you", "Let me honest with you" etc. It implies that you have been dishonest in the past and that does not help book gigs.

Congratulations! You Learned Some Great Fun Advisor Techniques!

Notes And Thoughts

Notes And Thoughts

Workshop 8 Fun With Negotiating

In this workshop I will teach you how to be an expert negotiator! Over the years, I've learned that negotiating with customers is more of an art than a science. There are many spokes to the wheel on this subject, so I'll share with you some of my favorite negotiating strategies. Crafting satisfactory price and terms with customers should be a fun and creative experience.

As covered earlier, being a friend first, building trust, lowering customer stress and asking the right questions are the main components to a great negotiator.

You could very well turn into a superstar negotiator by creating satisfactory win win solutions for everyone involved just by learning and practicing the techniques in this workshop. Have fun with this info and be on the lookout for more strategies to use as well.

Workshop Instructions:

1. Review the following strategies.

2. Try them out right away when speaking with customers.

3. Be on the lookout for more, there's plenty of books that have been written on the subject.

Negotiating Strategies

Asking For More- Ask for more than you expect because sometimes customers will say okay right out of the gate! Another advantage of starting off with a higher number is that it gives you some room to bargain. By offering a 20% discount...there should still be enough incentive for you to want the gig.

Bartering- Sometimes it makes sense to offer discounts to customers in exchange for using some of their services. We have bartered for things like advertising, gift certificates, movie tickets, waverunner rentals, golf games etc. so be on the look out for these kinds of opportunities.

Benefits Comment- Say something like this as a quick overview when discussing price, "Considering you'll have a lifetime of awesome memories, is [Amount] a fair rate?"

Big Ego Customers- You will from time to time run into a potential customer that likes to throw their ego around. The best way I've found to deal with this type of thing is to say something like, "Well, you're the expert, what do you think would be best in this situation?" Yielding to their ego will increase your chances of getting the gig.

Bracketing Statements- Sometimes you will be in a position where you have a high number and your potential customer has a low number. You might be satisfied with meeting in the middle. If so, say something like, "Can you meet me in the middle on that?" or, "How about we split the difference... Is that fair?"

Can You Guys Throw That In Too? – It's okay to ask for extra stuff because often they will agree to it. Make a concession request that seems over generous or perhaps borderline outrageous. You just might get it! Say something like "You'll throw in [What You Are Asking For] in on the deal, too right?".

Cheap Date Syndrome- I recommend that you do not fall into the cheap date category when quoting prices for your services. Once you are labeled a cheap date, it will take years to out live that reputation. Keep your rates at least in the middle range of your market or above.

Comment Positioning- If you offer a dollar amount to do a gig and the potential customer says, "That's too expensive!" simply reply with, "Well… let me ask you, how much too much do you think it is?" This lets you know what their magic number is… so you can decide if it's an acceptable amount.

Confidence Statement- "If you place your buying decision with us, you'll look like a party planning genius… hire the cheapest [Type Of Entertainment] in town and I'm not sure if you'll get the hugs and kisses from your guests that you want!"

Confidence Statement- "Based on everything I've heard so far…. we'd fit in perfectly with the festivities!"

Congratulations Statement- Congratulate your customer on making a wise buying decision when they say, "Okay, let's do it!

Customer Booking Preferences- Some people like to contact entertainment agencies when seeking talent while others prefer to surf the net and reach out to the artist directly. You should be well versed in both scenarios so that everyone involved in the process agrees that it is a pleasure doing business with you.

Flexibility With Customers- Some of your potential customers will be quick in deciding to hire you while others need some time to think it over. Offer them the flexibility to think things over yet entice them to place their buying decision with you as soon as possible because if they wait, you may not be available.

How Much Do You Charge?- When a potential customer asks you this question simply reply, "It depends on when, where and how long." You can then start filling out a hot lead sheet or collect their contact info and ask when it would be a good time to give them a call.

Investment Range- I love asking potential customers this question, "What's the most you want to invest on the music part of your [Type Of Event]?" or "What's a comfortable investment for you being that you are getting a wide range of quotes?" If they mention a number that is satisfactory to you simply say, "We can fulfill your needs for that!" If they mention a number that is not realistic or too low say, "Is there any way to get that number up? That's not a realistic rate for an expert."

Missed Opportunities- If you miss out on a gig, simply ask the customer if it was because of price or quality. Then ask for their permission to add them to your quarterly email list to at least have an opportunity to work with them next time. Most customers will be okay with allowing that.

Opening Statement- I have successfully started robust conversations with potential customers using this line, "I'm not sure if we are the right [Type Of Entertainment] for you so give us a call and let's find out!". Try it out and see if you get a potential customer to reach out to you.

Perceived Value- Perceived value is simply a customer's opinion of what your product or service is worth. If you're an expert at what you do, ask for expert fees.

Positioning Statement- If the customer will not tell you what their investment range is, say something like this, "On an average, we usually get [Dollar Amount] per hour, per musician. Then go over the benefits, "You get expert musicians, a great sounding speaker system, stage area lighting, set-up, tear down, unlimited music planning and a satisfaction guarantee. We also get together and have a rehearsal just for your event! Does that work for you?"

Powerful Negotiating Words- One of the most powerful words in negotiating is the word 'what'. If a potential customer throws out a low offer, simply say "WHAT?" Sometimes they will increase their offer.

Price Bumping- I have offered discounts to first time customers who do not want to pay my asking rate and then bump up the price each time they have me back. They happily pay more because they appreciate the quality and value I bring to the table. Try this strategy and see how it works for you.

Quoting Non-Round Numbers- When offering quotes, use non-round numbers like 597.00 instead of 600.00. It makes it seem like you have a formula behind what you are asking. Also, leave off the dollar sign on your numbers. The dollar sign is a symbol of cost, not gain.

Researching Customers- Most customers will shop around to get a feel for value because they do not want to be taken advantage of. They will disclose their findings if you ask them. Simply offer a satisfactory solution with great value so it's easy for them to place their buying decision with you.

Shopping Around Statement- Say this to your potential customer when you know they have not shopped around yet. "If you shop around, you will find prices are all over the map. The crazy expensive

[Entertainment Type] get [Dollar Amount] and the low quality [Entertainment Type] get [Dollar Amount]. We are in the middle range yet give you the finest quality! That's where the value is wouldn't you agree?".

Thanks Anyway Statement- If the numbers on a gig are not working you can say, "Unfortunately these numbers won't work for us but thank you for your consideration anyway."

This For That Negotiating- If you have a customer that is asking you to do something extra for them, simply say, "Okay, if we do that for you, what can you do for us?" A lot of times, they will quit asking for extra stuff that is outside of the parameters of what you have previously agreed to.

Venue Location- Knowing the special event location will let you know if a potential customer has financial resources. A potential customer having a wedding at an exclusive country club, in most cases, usually has more financial resources than someone renting out a small special event facility. Keep that in mind when putting together your proposals.

Win-Win Strategies- Successful negotiating is simply coming up with something that is satisfactory to all parties involved. Daily practice will get you real comfortable with the process.

Congratulations! You Learned Some Great Negotiating Strategies!

Notes And Thoughts

Notes And Thoughts

Workshop 9 Fun With Booking Gigs

In this workshop, I'll show you the eleven steps to a perfect gig along with four documents we use regularly. Getting paperwork over to the customer quickly, collecting deposits, gathering up event planners, showing up early on gig day, giving customers what they want and sending them a photo/video link of their party afterwards will give you the biggest chance of getting a great review.

This process gets us consistent 5-star reviews, so please take the time to learn the steps. You could very well turn into a 5-star junky... just like us!

Workshop Instructions:

1. Review and get familiar with the 11 steps to a perfect gig.

2. Create your version of a special event agreement and practice filling it out in under two minutes.

3. Create a script for emailing the filled-out agreement to customer.

4. Create a wedding ceremony and reception planner for your customers.

5. Create some live and DJ song lists so customers can select what tunes they want to hear.

6. Create a thank you script to email customer after the event.

7. Create a spreadsheet and add customers email for your quarterly e-blast.

11 Steps To A Perfect Gig!

1. Fill out a special event agreement

When your customer is ready to make a buying decision, fill out an agreement right away, there is a sample below for you to replicate. Have an attorney in your state look it over and give you the okay to use it. You should fill one out for every event to eliminate any possible miss-communication.

2. Email agreement and tune request/planners to customer

After you fill out the agreement, email it to them for their signature and ask them to email it back or drop it in the mail. Attach your tune request/planners to this email.

3. Have customer send in a deposit

Simply have your customer send in half of the total investment as a deposit.

4. Give your customer a courtesy call or email when the deposit arrives

This should be done before you deposit the funds.

5. Gather the tune requests and planners

Collect the tune requests and event planners several days before the gig.

6. Prep for the gig

The gig prep system, covered in workshop 10, is a must for every event and will keep your confidence level up.

7. Show up early

As covered in workshop 10, allow yourself plenty of extra time for unexpected travel delays. Ideally, your rig should be set up, sound checked and ready to go 30 minutes before the event starts.

8. Give the customer what they want

Play the tunes they requested and make the announcements they want.

9. Email them a thank you note along with a link to the photos and ask for a referral

Customers love photos of themselves having a great time so send them a thank you email (See Script Below) and include the photos link. It's also the perfect time to ask for a referral!

10. Email them a video link of their party

If you took some video footage, which I recommend you do, fly it into some editing software and create a short movie of the festivities.

11. Put the customer on your quarterly email list

Email your customers every three months so they will keep you in mind for their next special event. Always use proper etiquette by having some language at the end of your message giving them an opportunity to opt out of future emails if they so desire.

Next up is a special event agreement, email script for customers, and some wedding planners. Create your own version of each and start using them right away. Your customers will appreciate the organizational skills you possess.

Your Company Name

Agreement _____

THIS AGREEMENT, made this _____ day of _____,20___,between _____ (Hereinafter referred to as "Artist"), _____ (hereinafter referred to as "Purchaser") and **[Your Company Name]**.

It is mutually agreed between all parties as follows:
to the efforts of **[You Company Name]**, the employer hereby engages the Artist and the Artist hereby agrees to perform the engagement hereinafter provided upon all of the terms and conditions set forth herein.

(1) Type of event:

  (a) Location: _____

  Site contact/ph# _____
  (b) Date of Engagement: _____
  (c) Hours of Engagement: _____
  (d) Attire: _____
  (e) Total Investment: _____
  (f) Overtime: _____

(2) The Purchaser shall lock in talent by paying an Initial Investment of $ _____ to **[You Company Name]**, on or before the ____ day of _____, 20____.
Cash___ Check___ Pay Pal___

(3) The Purchaser shall pay the remainder of the Total Investment or _____ to **the Artist**,_____ , on or before
the ____day of _____,20 ____, as follows:

  Cash____ Check _____ Pay Pal _____
  By:_____

(4) If, at any time after the execution of this Agreement, either the Artist or the Purchaser should become unable to perform their obligations, as stated herein, due to conditions beyond their control, including but not limited to death, fire, or an Act of God, then this Agreement is cancelled and the initial investment shall be returned to the purchaser.

(5) This Agreement cannot be cancelled by either party without the consent and authorization of **[Your Company Name]**. In the event the Purchaser cancels without the consent of **[Your Company Name]**, the Agreement price shall become immediately due.

(6) The Purchaser shall at all times herein furnish the Artist with such facilities and services as are considered customary and adequate for the Artist's performance.

(7) **[Your Company Name]** to be held harmless from any liability arising from property damage or personal injury while providing the above services.

(8) This instrument constitutes the full Agreement between the parties, and any representation, statements or communications not specifically incorporated herein, shall not be binding or of any force or effect.

(9) The terms of this Agreement shall be construed to be severable, and if any portion thereof shall be declared invalid, then such invalidation shall not effect the remaining provisions of this Agreement and the same shall remain in full force and effect as if those such invalid provisions have been omitted.

(10) Failure of any party herein to enforce any of the terms or conditions of this Agreement shall not act as a waiver of obligation upon any of the other parties hereto in the future performance of any conditions covered by this Agreement.

(11) Purchaser shall provide the following:
  __ At least two (15A) 110V electrical outlets
  __ Stage/performance area _____ 'W x ____'D
  __ Rooms: Doubles _____ / Singles _____
  __ Food allowance of _____ Veggie___
  __ Beverage allowance of _____
  __ DJ Table_____
  __ Covering If Outside _____
  __ Other _____

ARTIST (S) AND PURCHASER CERTIFY THAT BY EXECUTING THIS AGREEMENT, THEY AGREE THAT IF ANY FUTURE ENGAGEMENTS ARE OBTAINED AS A RESULT OF THE ABOVE ENGAGEMENT, EITHER DIRECTLY OR INDIRECTLY, SAID ENGAGEMENT WILL FIRST BE REFFERED TO **[Your Company Name]**, FOR A PERIOD OF THIRTEEN MONTHS.

THIS AGREEMENT AND THE DEPOSIT MUST BE RECIEVED WITHIN FIVE CALENDER DAYS OR THIS ENGAGEMENT WILL BE CONSIDERED CANCELLED.

We, the undersigned, confirm that we have read and do hereby approve each and every term and condition set forth in this Agreement, this ___ day of _____, 20_____.

X_____
PURCHASER:

_____
ADDRESS / PHONE

ARTIST:_____

DAY OF EVENT CONTACT PHONE

[Your Company Name]
"Your motto or slogan"
[Your Name]   [Your Address]
web: [Your Web Site]   [City, State, Zip]
[Your Phone] (xxx) xxx-xxxx
[Your Email: xxx@xxxxxxxxx.com
Thank you for your business! We appreciate you!
©2018
Rick Sanford
HaveABlastBookingGigs.com

Sample Email Script For Customer (Once You Have Filled Out A Special Event Agreement)

Subject: Hi [Customers First Name], here's the agreement for [Date Of Event], please sign it and email it over or drop it in the mail.

Body:

I will give you a courtesy call or email when we receive the deposit.

Please send it to [Your Address].

Feel free to send us your tune requests anytime!

We like to get everything back from you no later than the Monday before the event.

I'll be giving you a call on the Monday or Tuesday before the big day for any final details you have for us!

Please call with any questions you might have.

Thank you for allowing us to be of service to you!

[Your Name And Phone Number]

Care to send your deposit via credit card?

Follow these simple instructions:

1. Go to [Your Website]

2. Click on the paypal button.

3. Enter in the amount of funds you wish to send in the item price box.

4. Click update.

5. Simply fill in your information.

6. Click the review and continue button.

7. Click the send funds button. Thank you, the funds have been sent!

Pick out your favorite tunes here: Online Interactive Song Search: [Your DJ Intelligence Link]

PS Practice your dance moves with this Evolution of Dance you tube video:

E-Z Wedding Ceremony Planner

Bride_____Groom_____

Date Of Wedding_____Time Guests Will Arrive_____

Location Address_____Ph#_____

Number In Wedding Party_____ bridemaids_____Mother/Grandmothers_____

Will This Event Be Inside Or Outside?_____

Name And Phone Number Of Coordinator_____

Name Of Officiant_____

WEDDING MUSIC SUGGESTIONS (Circle Your Choices)

Pre-Prelude (While Guests Are Arriving) We Typically Will Play Classical Music Or Email Over A List Of Your Favorite Love Songs.

Prelude (Seating Of The Mothers/Grandmothers/Bridal Party Entrance)	Composer
Jesu, Joy Of Man's Desiring	Bach
Largo	Handel
Air	Handel

Other_____

Processional (Brides Entrance)
Bridal Chorus	Wagner
Trumpet Voluntary	Clarke
Canon In D	Pachelbel

Other_____

Ceremony (Optional)
Ave Maria	Schubert
The Wedding Song (There Is Love)	Stookey

Other_____

Recessional (Bride & Groom Exit)
Wedding March	Mendelssohn
Hornpipe In D	Handel
Trumpet Tune (Martial Air)	Purcell

Other_____

Thank You & Congratulations! Please Email This Info Over To [Your Email] At Least Five Days Prior To Your Event. Questions? Please Call [your phone number] Anytime!

E-Z Wedding Reception Planner

The Bride And Groom Are To Be Introduced As: _____

Date: _____ Location_____

Ph # of Reception Site: _____ Contact Person: _____

*Some couples like to have the wedding party announced. If so, fill in their names in the order you wish for them to be introduced. Is there a special tune you want played?

Bride's Father: _____ Bride's Mother: _____

Groom's Father: _____ Groom's Mother: _____

(Maid, Matron) Of Honor: _____ Bestman: _____

Bridesmaid: _____ Groomsmen: _____

Bridesmaid: _____ Groomsmen: _____

Bridesmaid: _____ Groomsmen: _____

Bridesmaid: _____ Groomsmen: _____

Bridesmaid: _____ Groomsmen: _____

Flower Girl: _____ Ringbearer: _____

*Would you like the wedding party to form a semi-circle around the dance floor for your 1st dance or take a seat? _____

1) Bride & Grooms 1st Dance_____ Artist: _____ Nod2Fade

2) Father/Daughter Dance: _____ Artist: _____ Nod2Fade

3) Mother/Son Dance_____ Artist: _____ Nod2Fade

4) Bridal Party Dance_____ Artist: _____

5) Other Dances_____ Artist: _____

Announcements

___ Announcement of Wedding Party

___ First Dance   Immediately following the introduction? Yes / No

Would you like the other specialty dances played right after the bride and groom dance? Yes / No

Please let us know which of these you would like.

___Toast

___Cake Cutting

___Bouquet Toss**

___Garter Toss**

___Marraige Dance***

___Money Dance

___Last Dance

___Blessing Given By _____

Person To Notify Us On Anouncements/Timeline: _____

**During the bouquet/ garter toss, the photographer will usually want to take a staged shot…after the staged shot, we will play a drum roll and count to three!

***The Marriage Dance is something fun to do if you would like to. We invite all married couples to the dance floor for a slow tune and then peel away the couples in accordance to how long they have been married. We start with 2 hours, 1 year, 5 years, 10 years, 20 years, etc… the couple who's been married the longest gets a big applause! ☺

Thanks & Congratulations! Please share with us any other comments, requests or suggestions for your perfect wedding day:

Please email this planner over to [your email] at least five days prior to your event. Questions? Please call [your phone number] anytime!

Notes And Thoughts

Notes And Thoughts

Workshop 10 Fun With Gig Prep And Execution

In this workshop, I will show you how to be a gig prep and execution expert so you can ace every special event that comes along your way.

There's seven main sections I will share with you. Being that I am a systems guy and manager for our band, I kept working on ways to organize the many details associated with gig prep, rehearsal and gig execution so all the moving parts could run as smooth as possible.

The following gig profile, playlist creation steps, rehearsal workflow, gig prep checklist, personal logistics timeline, post gig report and customer rockumentary were all designed to keep details in order so that I wouldn't miss anything.

If you create and follow some systems like these, you've demonstrated what I call extra effort. That's what separates the experts from everyone else. You could very well end up being one of the best in the industry at serving customers and earning a ton of 5-star reviews.

Workshop Instructions:

1. Study the gig prep and execution strategies below.

2. Create your own version of the gig profile.

3. Try out the playlist creation and rehearsal strategy before your next gig.

4. Work up a gig prep checklist.

5. Create a personal logistics timeline.

6. Create a post gig report.

7. Create a customer rockumentary checklist.

Gig Prep And Execution Strategies

Announcements And Introductions- Announcements and introductions should be practiced the day before the gig if possible. This lowers any stress or anxiety that might arise. Make sure you are pronouncing names correctly by running them buy the customer first.

Business Cards- Of course plan on handing out a bunch of business cards to as many people as possible and let them know you offer referral fees. If you are working with an agent/manager, ask them for their cards and hand those out instead of yours.

Collect Email Addresses And Business Cards- Collect as many emails as possible by telling folks you will email them the group shot. Also ask the vendors for their card as well including the venue contact, coordinator, photographer, audio engineer etc. so you can put them on your quarterlye-blast.

Confirm A Gig Procedure With Band Mates- If you fill out an agreement and email it to the customer, email a tentative message to your band mates so they know about it. When you receive the deposit from the customer, send out a confirmation email to your band mates so they know to put it on their calendar. You should also let them know when and where the rehearsal is.

Drinking Policy- Make sure everyone you work with agrees to a two-drink max if the customer insists the band partake in alcoholic beverages. This policy will save you some gigs. Let everyone in the band know that intoxication is never allowed. It takes 20 years to build a great reputation and 20 seconds to destroy it.

Extra Mics- It's good to have an extra mic hooked up as a back up or for when a special guest might drop by to sing a tune.

Filling In With Other Bands- It's a joy filling in as a sub with other bands and it can really broaden your musical horizons. Ask the music director for the list of tunes, what key they play them in and any audio/video references available, so you can map out their show. Always be willing to rehearse with them as well.

Flyers- Print up some flyers and hand them out to folks at your gigs. It's inexpensive yet effective promotional material.

Ghost Tracks- If you are playing pre-recorded music anytime during your show, have a ghost track running in case your primary audio source dies on you. It does and will happen so be ready to bring in the secondary audio source in a moment's notice!

Identify Yourself- Having a sign or banner on stage with your band name on it is a must. Let the audience know who you are so they can find you online and hopefully hire you for an event!

Laptop Prep – Your laptops or audio sources should be updated/prepped the day before the gig to make sure your tune catalog is indexed and ready to go.

Management- Great managers know that what gets measured, gets done so using systems like the one's in this workshop will solve a lot of challenges in keeping a band together and performing at optimal levels.

Management- Being soft on people and hard on solutions is the mark of a great management system.

Overtime Procedure- As we all know, time flies when you're having fun so ask your customer a few minutes before the end time if they would like to keep the party going. If they do, offer your services in thirty minute intervals so they can decide how long to keep the celebration going.

Outdoor Gigs- Make sure you ask for a tent or some type of covering if your gig is outside. No gig is worth ruining your gear over.

Playlist Creation- Collect the tune requests from the customer and create a playlist before rehearsal so you can go down it in order working on smooth starts, stops and transitions.

Preferred Vendors- Getting on a preferred vendor list can generate a lot of gigs. Some venues have them so inquire about how to get on it. Of course, offer referral fees to them if they get you a gig.

Recognizing Bar Staff- Performing in a nightclub or restaurant? Write down the bartenders and waitresses names and mention them at least once per set. They will love you for it! Say something like this,

"Folks, please take care of your bartenders and waitresses! They are working awfully hard for you tonight! We have, (Mention Their Names)".

Recording Your Shows- I recommend recording your shows so you can go back and review your performances. It's the best way to identify and smooth out any rough spots.

Rehearsal Importance- The biggest reasons to have a rehearsal is quality control and an opportunity to for the band to gel. Professional bands rehearse so always plan a rehearsal.

Rip-Off Alert- If anyone rips you off, have an attorney send them a letter requesting payment. If that doesn't work, drag them to court and get your money. It's that simple.

Show Enders- End your show with a bang! Create some for your show today!

Smile When It Hurts- Hit a wrong note or chord, smile when it hurts!

Song Grid- I recommend creating a sharable doc, aka a song grid, for your band so you can document how you do all your tunes. Title, artist, YouTube link, key, instrumentation, arrangement, chord chart and lyrics can all be logged so there is never any question on how the tunes are performed.

Song List/Tip Strategy- Performing in a public place? I've done a ton of restaurant and nightclub gigs over the years and have had great success making tips by printing up my song list and putting them in my tip bucket. I'd invite folks up to the stage to grab one and they really loved being able to call out a tune... and leave a nice tip.

Sound Reinforcement/Lighting- If you are working with an outside audio-visual company, give them up to date changes on your input list and stage plot. Don't throw them a curve ball on gig day. They will appreciate the fact that you gave them a heads up!

Specialty Dances At Weddings- What's the perfect length to a specialty dance? Let the bride and groom, father daughter/mother son dancers decide by having one of them give you a nod when they want you to end or fade out the music.

Stagehands- Stagehands are the unsung heroes of the industry! They should be trained properly before the gig. Create some training instructions on everything that needs to be done and share it with them. A great stagehand unloads gear, assists in setting up the lights and sound system, locates fuse boxes, takes pictures/videos throughout the evening, provides security, hands out business cards and helps on load out.

Time Management Strategy- Expert time management is being ready one hour before you must leave for a gig. This prevents hurry sickness and should be practiced by everyone.

Traffic Considerations- Plan on there being a traffic jam on the way to every gig. Having an alternate route to the gig is also a good idea.

Vocal Techniques- When introducing folks or making announcements, pretend you are a radio personality. Avoid speaking too fast and keep your voice moving around in the low, middle and hi registers to keep it interesting for the listeners.

Wedding Ceremony/Reception Planners- Collect the music and announcement info from your customer several days before the event. This will allow you to get a jump on the prep work because the more prepared you are, the higher your confidence level will be. On gig day, have a checklist to help you keep track of everything that's supposed to happen. It's easy to forget things when you are caught up in the festivities.

Wedding Coordinators- I recommend doing everything possible to please the wedding coordinator. It's okay to offer suggestions about fun things to do at weddings but allow them to decide what's best. If you do a great job, they will recommend you to other customers and of course they get a referral fee.

Wedding Reception Fun- Ask the bride and groom to come up to the stage, put some guitars on them and take some pictures! It's always a hit!

Gig Prep 1: The Gig Profile

The gig profile has seven sections to it and covers just about everything your band would need to know about a gig. The seven sections are talent line up, rehearsal date, event details, gig day timeline, tune requests/event activities, playlist creation and a fine print section for band policies or boundaries you may wish to share. If you post this info on a sharable doc and invite everyone on the gig to join it, they'll have a complete rundown of the gig details.

Gig Profile (Page 1 of 3)

Event#:

Private Event=No Guests (Make Sure Everyone Knows This)

Talent Line Up:

[Whose On The Gig]

Stagehand:

Rehearsal- [Date Time Location].

Rehearsal workflow:

Jam session (originals or covers)

New cover tunes you want to try out

Customer requests

Event Details:

Who:

What:

Where:

When:

Why:

How:

Venue Contact Person:

Dock Master:

Wedding Coordinator:

Inside/Outside:

Attire:

Green Room/Change:

Stash Cases:

Gig Profile (Page 2 of 3)

Day Of Event Timeline

Meet:

Leave:

Set Up Crew:

Back Line Call Time:

Front Line Call Time:

Full Band Sound Check:

Clear:

Change:

Food Allowance:

Band Photo At Stage:

Play Time:

Strike It Unless Overtime:

Leave for home:

Tune Requests And Event Activities

*Wedding Party Introduction Tune-

*First Dance-

*Father Daughter Dance-

*Mother Son Dance-

*Other Dances-

*Marriage Dance-

*Toast Given By-

*Cake Cutting-

*Bouquet Toss-

*Garter Toss-

*Last Dance-

Playlist Creation:

Create a playlist of the customer requests. At rehearsal, our band makes it a habit of going over the following criteria for each tune the customer wants to hear so there is zero slop on the stage. For each tune we go over:

How it starts, key/tempo/groove, correct arrangement, whose singing lead, whose got back-up vocals, who solos and how it ends.

Reference Tools: [Share YouTube Links Of The Tunes You Are Doing For Reference]

Song Grid Link: [Share Your Song Grid Link That Opens A Sharable Doc Showing Everyone How The Tunes Will Be Played]

Gig Profile (Page 3 of 3)

Fine Print:

Nobody likes rules, but everyone is okay with systems that makes sense so create some boundaries your band mates all agree to. Let everyone know up front what great performance looks like, ask for some feedback and suggestions they might have as well. They will appreciate you asking them and will be thankful that you are considerate toward their needs as well.

Here are some things you may wish to consider for your bands fine print section. Every band has boundaries, what are yours?

*Please create and use a load up checklist for your gear and attire.

*Time Management- Please add a minimum 25% travel time buffer and have a couple of routes to the gig...PLAN ON TRAFFIC BEING BAD. Expert time management is the mark of a pro.

*Please warm up your voice with googs and guugs on the way to the gig.

*Please color code/tag your cords, stands etc. so that everyone leaves with what they came with.

*Cautions & Security: Safety first please! Also, please see to it that no gear falls, breaks, gets lost or stolen. We need everyone to be careful. pay attention and watch the gear.

*Please do not disappear until after sound check. We need a 'thumbs up' from everybody at sound check.

*Please keep any music stands flat so the audience can see you.

*Please sign off on each tune arrangement/groove we are playing.

*Please see to it that the ladies in the band are escorted to and from their vehicles.

*Please know the next song before the current one ends. Dead time elimination is a great thing!

*The person singing lead shall queue any additional solos.

*We are ladies and gentlemen serving ladies and gentlemen.

*Please install _new_ batteries in all gear before each gig.

*Please refrain from using inappropriate language while at the venue.

*Mistakes? Smile when it hurts! Smile a lot anyway, we're onstage!

*As a courtesy, please leave the stage area like you found it, thank you!

*Please Pray For & Support Our Troops! They make all this possible. [End Of Gig Profile]

Gig Prep 2 Playlist Creation

1. Gather the requests from the customer.

2. Determine what singers will be on the stage.

3. Create a playlist giving each singer some coverage.

4. Get the bands okay on the playlist.

5. Run down the playlist at rehearsal.

Gig Prep 3 Rehearsal Workflow

1. Start off the rehearsal with a jam session of original grooves and tunes for 20 minutes or so. Perhaps start building an original music catalog.

2. Rehearse any specialty tunes the customer wants to hear.

3. Go over the following 7 criteria for each tune on the play list: Who starts it, key/tempo/groove, correct arrangement, whose singing/whose got back-up vocals, who solos, how's it end, dead time elimination.

Gig Prep 4 The Gig Prep Checklist

Create a list of everything you need to do before the gig. Here's an example:

Create a gig profile on Google Drive and invite band mates

Collect tune requests/planners from customer with balance reminder

Create band playlist/ rehearse show with band in playlist order

Call venue for load in instructions

Pick up any rental gear (lights, etc.)

Pick up supplies (guitar strings, confetti, and inflatable's)

Check/prep gear

Train stagehand

Wash vehicle

Go over tunes/charts

Load up the truck/trailer (using your gear check list)

Change strings

Print playlists

Write checks to talent

Inflatable's/confetti canon

Scrolling sign programmed

Create input/monitor list (see next page)

Charge batteries on camera/video camera and delete memory card data

Prep laptops and load back up gear: Speakers, power amps, etc.

Gift for customer

Audio Visual Input List For The Gig

Whip up one of these before each gig so setup is a little easier:

Channel Assignment

1 2 3 4 5 6 7 8 9 10 11 12 13 14 15 16 aux in

Lighting   1   2   3   4   with controller

Monitor Assignment (Create one before each gig)

aux1   aux2   aux3   aux4   aux5   aux6

Monitor Requests?

(If you can, get this before the gig so you can dial in everything quicker.)

Band Member 1-

Band Member 2-

Band Member 3-

Band Member 4-

Band Member 5-

Band Member 6-

Gig Prep 5 Personal Logistics Timeline

Here's an example of the one I use. I start at the bottom of the list and work my way up. Create one for your needs. Avoid playing the hurry sickness game.

Prep Clothes:

Change Strings:

Load Up:

Nap:

Stretch Out:

Shower:

Eat:

Instrument Warm Up:

Depart For Venue:

Arrive At Venue:

Set Up By:

The Post Gig Report

Create a list of things you would like to evaluate after an event and give yourself a grade:

Gig Overall Grade:

What Went Great?

What Needs Attention?

Appearance:

Audience Engagement:

Clipboard To Capture Emails:

Cooperation With Other Vendors:

Correct Arrangements:

Correct Key Starts:

Correct Starts:

Customer Service At Event:

Customer Service Internet:

Customer Service Phone:

Dead Time Elimination:

Element Of Surprise:

Gift For Customer:

Grand Big Bang Exit:

Group Shot:

Handling Requests:

Introductions:

Introduce Band Members:

Invite Folks To Facebook

Lighting/FX:

Overall Show Mojo:

Pass Out Business Cards:

Picture With Customer:

Rig Appearance:

Song Dynamics:

Smile Factor:

Sound Quality:

Time Management And Promptness:

Volume Levels On Comp And Solos:

Did Everyone Have A Blast?

The Customer Rockumentary

Customers love it when you send them a thank you email with links to the photos/videos you took of their special event. It's the perfect time to ask for a review as well. Make sure you do this to start building your 5-star reviews up.

Here are the steps we take:

1. Crop the party photos you took and upload them to your photo sharing site, create an album and generate a sharable link.

2. Send a thank you email within 24 hours to the customer, add the party photos link and ask for a referral. (See thank you email script in workshop 4)

3. Fly any videos that you have taken into your editing software and create a short video of the special event. Upload it to your video sharing site and create a shareable link and email it to the customer.

4. Add customers email to your quarterly eblast list.

5. Post your party group shot on your website and blog.

Congratulations! You Learned Some Great

Gig Prep & Execution Strategies!

Well that's it! The A Blast Cycle Of Awesome... 30 years of fun tied into ten workshops. I hope and pray that this book helps you become one the best in the industry at serving your community! It's been an honor and privilege teaching you this stuff, thank you for reading it. Stay Blessed, Stay Blast!

Notes And Thoughts

Notes And Thoughts

Resources

I've used a lot of great products and services over the years and here's a list of some of them. Let us know if you run across some we should know about, so we can get the word out.

Audio Sharing- soundcloud.com

Banner Creation- puresilvabannermaker.com

Business Cards- vistaprint.com

Cloud Data Sharing- dropbox.com

Computer Data Backup- backblaze.com

Domain Registration- godaddy.com

E-book Cover Maker- myecovermaker.com

Graphics Generator- cooltext.com

Guitar Recording Software- sonomawireworks.com/riffworks

Karaoke Online- karafun.com

Music Search- djintelligence.com

Labels To I.D. Gear- buck.com/labels

Legal Representation- legalshield.com

Liability Insurance- theeventhelper.com

Logo Design- logomaker.com

Music Subscription Service- promoonly.com

Original Music Website- bandzoogle.com (Visit blast-tracks.com if you want to check out our original music catalog.)

Recognition Engraving & Awards- awardshere.com

Trademark Attorney- Lee Beitchman Beitchman & Hudson, LLP

Video Editing Software- movavi.com

Video Services & Streaming- videovg.com

Voicemail- voiceconnectinc.com

Website- wordpress.org

Website Design- elegantimagestudios.com

About The Author

Photo Credit: Brian Stephens

Rick Sanford is a successful musician, entrepreneur, and teacher. He is founder of A Blast Bands And DJs®, guitarist and co-founder of The Blast Band® and author of the Have A Blast Booking And Performing Gigs training programs.

Rick and team have spent 30 years serving thousands of customers needing musical entertainment for their special events and has created a system that consistently produces 5-star reviews.

After collecting years of knowledge, wisdom and experience, Rick decided to create ten powerful self-help workshops called the A Blast

Cycle Of Awesome so that every musician can learn how to quickly become an expert at booking and performing gigs.

Rick says, "Musicians/creative types are different than normal people; we think differently and thus need special tools and strategies to help us get the most out of our time, talents and resources."

Rick believes this book should be in every musician's toolbox because it shows them how to be more successful personally and professionally. Rick invites you to take advantage of this information by completing the workshop assignments and capture the many benefits each have to offer.

Ricks favorite motto is, "It's fun being successful!" This book was written to inspire, train and motivate musicians so that they too can go forth, serve and Have A Blast!

Questions or comments?

Email Rick at rick@haveablastpublishing.com or find me on the following social networks:

Facebook: fb.me/gigbookingsecrets

YouTube: http://www.youtube.com/haveablastbookinggigs

More From This Author

Rick is offering additional training, coaching and business opportunities. Visit us online at GigBookingSecrets.com for further information.

One Last Thing...

Please take a moment to rate this book. If you believe the book is worth sharing, please let your friends know about it. If it turns out to make a difference in their lives, they'll be forever grateful to you, as will I.

Special Thanks To

God Almighty for giving us music and talents to develop.

My lovely wife Jennifer, my parents, Charles and Bonnie Sanford, my three sisters Karen, Lisa and Judy, the Lott Family Jerry, Christine, Jeff, Greg and Aimee Lott, as well as Lexie Neal for the years of support.

Robert Hinton Photodesign for the book cover artwork.

The sensational Kris Tonner, co-founder of The Blast Band®, for showing up at the perfect time and having 22 years of great times serving others.

Dave Allen for the rock-solid drumming.

Darren Rogers for being an outstanding creative contributor to the band singing, composing and performing.

Sherita and Sherie Murphy along with all the Blastettes for doing an amazing job on the front line singing and dancing.

Ollie Patterson and the Big Blast Horn Section.

Robert Meadows for the talent you bring to the table.

Kevin Wyglad for his musicianship and talent recommendations.

Brad Hammock, Duncan Elrod, Dean Tomlinson, John Schmitz, Mike Keaveny and all the stagehands we've had the pleasure of working with over the years! Thank you for saving our backs!

Wendy Whitehead for being a great administrative assistant.

All the great musicians, bands, DJ's, band managers, agents, sound engineers and promoters we've had the pleasure of working with including Jeff Pike, Conner Lorre, Rick Austin, Sid Wolf, Chris Hibbert, Betty Seni, Ron Adwaters, Mike Force, Jim Tidwell, Robby Heisner, Danny Garrett, Phil Fontana, Jim Boling, Greg Smith, Linda Walker, Toric Smith, Beth Michaels, John Davis, Chuck Bithorn, Jay Fink, George Calhoun, Gil Estes, Jeff Gillman, Rich Leverone, Danny Fossett, Tony Delamont, Clay Musgrave, Nick Longo, Bill Pound, Sean O'Rourke, Bill Shirk, Mike Byrne, Keith Evans, Steve Pace, Bobby Hendrix, Jimmy Mouton, Dave Midkiff, Mark Ledford, Brian Stephens, East Coast Entertainment, Mathew DiBennedetto, Ricky Fargo, Don McBroom, Jeff Yackel, Danny Ray Cole, Mark Strickland, Roger Smith, KC Cass, Ned Sudreth, George Sandler, Pro South Entertainment, Richie Mays, Eric Snipes, Mike Tarpley, Johnny Duncan, Glow Band, Bullettproof Band, Dennis Smith and Party On The Moon, Russ Rogers, Wally Tirado, Louis Van Dora, Wendell Holmes Jr., Don Hacker, Michael Todd, Derrick Huff, Wallace Reed and Joel Rabe at Lethal Rhythms.

All the great customers we've had the pleasure of serving including Cliff Kinsey at Children's Restoration Network, Clark And Neel Bennett at Sharkys Beach Bar, Justin Hendricks, Ray Hornsby, Michele D. Hornsby, Sandy Lamm, Pauly D, Caliber Promotions, Mark Henry, Ray Barker, David DP Preshel, Francis Starr at Head Start Region IV, ADTRAV Corp., Kelly Saad at Vistar of Atlanta, Roger Abbott at Dental TLC, High Meadows School, Lake Lanier Sailing Club, Kristine Knipp at Atlanta Ballroom Dancers, Lavada Herman at ComSouth, Donna Hand at Athens Country Club and Global Connections.

It has been an amazing 30+ years, thank you... I'd do it all over again! ☺

www.ingramcontent.com/pod-product-compliance
Lightning Source LLC
Chambersburg PA
CBHW070945230426
43666CB00011B/2573